LIFE BEHIND BARS

To my grandmother, with much love and admiration.

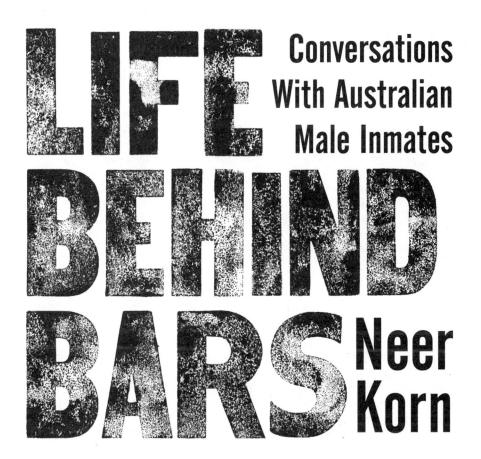

LIFE BEHIND BARS

Conversations With Australian Male Inmates

Neer Korn

NEW
HOLLAND

First published in Australia in 2004 by
New Holland Publishers (Australia) Pty Ltd
Sydney • Auckland • London • Cape Town

14 Aquatic Drive Frenchs Forest NSW 2086 Australia
218 Lake Road Northcote Auckland New Zealand
86 Edgware Road London W2 2EA United Kingdom
80 McKenzie Street Cape Town 8001 South Africa

National Library of Australia Cataloguing-in-Publication Data:

Korn, Neer.
Life behind bars: conversations with Australian male
inmates.

Includes index.
ISBN 1 74110 094 1.

1. Prisoners - Australia - Interviews. 2. Prisons -
Australia. I. Title.

365.440994

Publishing Manager: Robynne Millward
Project Editors: Claire de Medici and Liz Hardy
Designer: Karlman Roper
Production Manager: Linda Bottari
Printed in Australia by McPherson's Printing Group, Victoria

10 9 8 7 6 5 4 3 2 1

A society should be judged not by how it treats its outstanding citizens but by how it treats its criminals.

Fyodor Dostoyevsky

Neer Korn is a director of social market research company, Hearbeat. His writing has been published in newspapers and magazines across Australia and he is frequently asked to speak and commentate on social trends and issues. He can be contacted by email at neer@heartbeat.com.au.

Neer Korn is also the author of *Shades of Belonging: Conversations with Australian Jews.*

Acknowledgments

There are a number of people whose assistance and support I am grateful for.

Thank you to Lawrence Goodstone for pointing me in the right direction and offering years' worth of experience; the ever efficient and knowledgeable Bob Stapleton from the Department of Corrective Services' PR office; and Rachel Haggett, the passionate and determined director of the Violence Prevention Program. These three people were instrumental in bringing this project to fruition.

Thank you to Professor Tony Vinson for his advice, Diane Moy for her research and Dominika Ferenz for the photographs used in this book.

Thank you to Tara Wynne from Curtis Brown for her guidance and to Robynne Millward, Claire de Medici and Liz Hardy at New Holland for sharing my passion for this project.

Thank you also to Jason, David, Michael, Darren, Shane, Stuart and Gordon for sharing their stories.

Finally, thank you to those around me with whom I relentlessly shared my thoughts while writing this book.

Contents

Prologue

The origins of this book can be traced back to a very late night in a tiny smoke-filled all-night cafe in Kings Cross. While sipping on a second or third latte with a friend, I relayed my experiences from earlier that day at Sydney's Long Bay Prison complex.

I had been to see an inmate, Peter Schneidas, who was serving a life sentence for the 1979 murder of a prison officer (a crime committed while Schneidas was incarcerated for writing bad cheques and later attacking another prison officer). At the time, I was exploring the idea of writing a book about the role of religion in the lives of prisoners, and had been speaking with prison chaplains who ministered Schneidas. I did not know that Schneidas was one of the state's most notorious inmates, whose treatment in prison led to a fifty-seven-day hunger strike and, in part, to a royal commission into the state's corrective services.

Schneidas left little impression on me that morning in the concreted yard of the minimum-security prison at the top of the Long Bay complex. He did not say much and seemed to be in extreme discomfort, repeatedly asking for help in treating a chronic back problem.

The visit was not as eye-opening as I had hoped but it did offer me a glimpse of the menacing nature of prison: grey metal bars, large swinging locks and the constant presence of empowered blue-uniformed officers and incarcerated green-clothed inmates. Most prison-like, perhaps, were the intermittent and intrusive noises that formed the backdrop to our conversation: locks clanging, bells ringing and intercom bellowing. I felt like I had been on a tour of the set of the 1980s television program *Prisoner*.

Having exhausted both the story and my caffeine intake, I stood to leave the cafe, when a stocky, white-haired man in his late forties sitting at the next table asked, 'Were you talking about Peter Schneidas?' I nodded, and he continued, 'I thought I heard you right. Well, I know him. Me and him, you see, we used to write to each other, played chess through our letters'. It turned out that the two had served time in prison together. 'I was there in the wing when he killed the prison officer. Anyway, when I got out I felt sorry for him, being in solitary and that, so we'd write [to] each other, making chess moves and talking about stuff. That began ten years ago ... I've got most of the letters he's sent me. You can have them if you like.'

Sure enough, several days later I dropped into the cafe and found a large envelope filled with handwritten and typed white and yellow lined pages waiting for me. I began reading the first letter and it was not until hours later that I left the cafe, having read the last. I was impressed by how articulate Schneidas was, considering his limited schooling; I later learnt that while incarcerated he had completed his secondary school education and some subjects towards a law degree. He was able to convey the self-examination that perpetually occupied his time, and to do so with clarity and insight. Schneidas's letters were filled with raw descriptions of prison life, his living conditions and the extremities of his emotional state. Schneidas's words told of a world I had read about in books and seen in films and on television but had not personalised.

Following is a letter from early March 1986:

I'm now in worse conditions than I've been in since I was seventeen and in Grafton—and that's really saying something.

I was thrown over boxes, punched, my spine has snapped out again and I'm supposed to ignore it and pretend it never happened. I can't do that. If I did it would be saying that the screws can bash me and it's okay. It's hypocrisy and it's worse because it reinforces violence. That might sound a bit strange coming from someone of my history but violence really is the weak man's way of reacting to things. It's taken me many, many years to realise that. I've been bashed and abused for twenty years because I was violent. My violence was used as the excuse to heap violence on me. I was told that violence was antisocial and if I used violence I had to accept the consequences of it. The consequence was prison and more violence.

These men must also accept the consequences of their violence, not through more violence but through the law. If the system condemns violence then it must also condemn the violence of its own people; if it doesn't, then the whole thing becomes no more than a joke, it becomes no more than people grasping for power and doing everything they think they must do to hold on to it. When I would strike out it was always from an emotional base. I'd been wounded and I fought back in the only way the system had taught me to. But their violence is cold-blooded, calculated. It's rational and that makes it dangerous.

My interest now sparked, I started making some phone calls and soon found myself speaking with Schneidas's wife, whom he had married in prison eight years earlier—the two met while Schneidas was studying for a law degree and corresponding with the legal centre where she worked. Shortly after our phone conversation, I was given

Peter Schneidas's entire file: two over-packed manila folders filled with papers including legal submissions, reports and judgments.

From this package and Schneidas's letters I learnt that Peter Schneidas was born in Lithuania in August 1957. His parents divorced before his first birthday and he spent many of his early years in state-run boarding schools before migrating to Australia with his mother and sister in 1965. He did not settle well into school life here and spent many months in and out of boys' homes as punishment for truancy. According to a court submission written by his wife, Schneidas stated that he began to truant because he could not speak English, which led to his being considered dull by his teachers and being tormented by his fellow students.

In 1975, at age seventeen, Schneidas was sentenced to eight months imprisonment for writing bad cheques and was sent to Grafton, an adult prison that housed the state's most hardened criminals. Until now, his wife stated in the submission, Schneidas had not exhibited violent behaviour and said it was here he was taught that violence was the appropriate—and only—way of dealing with the world around him.

Upon arrival, Schneidas was treated to Grafton's infamous 'reception biff', which was condemned for its brutality and human rights abuse by the Nagle Royal Commission into New South Wales Prisons some years later, and is no longer practised. The aim of the reception biff was to break inmates physically and mentally in order to assert status. In the memoirs he began writing in prison, *And Not to Yield*, Schneidas described the experience:

I walk through the cell door and a screw hits me across the nose with the edge of his hand. My nose bleeds.

There are four other screws with batons ... They hit me with their batons, all of them. On my knees, my back, my hands, my head. I fall. I begin to scream. I beg. I grovel. The slap of the batons on my body, the crack of my bones and my own screaming are all I can hear. I stop resisting. I can't move.

I try to get up, stumbling. They kick me. I fall. They kick me again. I crawl. There's blood everywhere ... I crawl to a corner, roll into a ball trying to protect myself. I am afraid and screaming. Whimpering. Begging. They keep beating me as if they're trying to bury me in the corner. I am crying. Tears. Sobbing. They stop. I see shoes and trouser legs leave the cell. That's all I see. The uniforms. The batons. They had belted me to a pulp. I was humiliated by my own weakness, by my own vulnerability in the face of sheer physical force. I hated myself for my weaknesses and I hated them for exposing it ...

The guys in the yard laughed at me about how I'd responded to my reception biff. They ribbed me about crying out and screaming. To make noise at your reception biff was to be weak. I never accepted that code of silence when being flogged. The quieter you were, the easier you made it for them. Bellow, I thought. Scream and rage as loudly as you can because if you're silent they can't [can] pretend you don't exist. They can pretend that you're a thing and not a human being. Your humanity is your voice. Use it. Roar it. I am here and I exist.[1]

Over time, Schneidas became a violent inmate, particularly towards prison officers, and received a further ten-year sentence for a violent assault of a guard. Then, one day in August 1979, as the inmates were sitting down to their evening meal at 3 pm, Schneidas attacked prison officer John Mewburn, killing him with eight blows of a hammer.

After the ensuing court case and just prior to sentencing, Schneidas told his psychiatrist, William Barclay:

> *I am twenty years old. I have been beaten and I have been given the reputation for violence. I have never had a go—I have never been given a decent job in jail. I admit I have hit back and I have done some things to get me into trouble, but I have never been violent outside of jail—only inside in response to the way I have been treated. You get so you despise authority. I have tried to behave myself in jail, but it gets me nowhere. They won't give me a chance—there is no way I can get a fair go in the jail. I am not looking for trouble—I try to avoid it. I have a bad reputation and things just go from bad to worse in jail.[2]*

When Schneidas was sentenced to life imprisonment, prison officers revolted, refusing to house him in the general prison population. Consequently, he spent almost four years in solitary confinement, a form of incarceration designed for short periods only. Sydney barrister John Baste visited Schneidas at this time and described his living conditions, noting that the unit:

> *... consists of two sets of yards on either side of a corridor. On the right-hand side as one enters it are the small yards. These appear to be approximately two paces across and ten paces deep. They have solid metal doors with a food trap which can only be opened from the outside. It was impossible to see out ... I am told that during winter when the temperature*

is well below zero, a small amount of sunshine may be obtained in the small yards; however the walls are bare concrete approximately ten or twelve feet high ... They remind me of old-fashioned animal yards in zoos. Indeed, I believe that description to be flattering. I cannot recall visiting a zoo in which an animal was kept in such a small confine.[3]

Schneidas's letters from this period show his increasing despondency and he wrote:

I am still in solitary confinement. How can I help but act to that with despair? I'm at the end of the line. I have no recourse. It's not the officers that I have trouble handling; it's the isolation. It magnifies everything. It distorts the things you perceive and the ways in which you react. An order shouted at me becomes a personal attack. A plate of food thrown at me becomes an expression of scorn and contempt. I don't expect officers to like me. I don't even expect them to treat me with courtesy. I expect them to go about the business of doing their job and I expect them to be professional. I just see past their uniforms and recognise the person underneath. In the same way, I expect them to recognise my humanity. I'm desperately fighting my past, trying to break out of the cycle. Perhaps I'm being unrealistic in expecting them to recognise this, let alone help me. But I can't do it alone. I need help. If someone treated you the way I'm treated, you'd dismiss them from your life. I don't have that option.

In desperation, Schneidas began his second and longest hunger strike in 1983, seeking an end to his isolation. The strike continued for fifty-seven days amid much publicity, inspiring Don Chipp, then a Victorian Senator and later the founder of the Australian Democrats, to write to NSW Premier Neville Wran that 'No human being should be submitted to such unfair and discriminatory treatment continuously. Such treatment is horrific enough in countries with a poor human rights record; it's an absolute disgrace to hear of this occurring in Australia'.[4] The hunger strike ended when an agreement to integrate Schneidas into the general prison population was reached.

The early 1980s were a controversial time for the New South Wales Department of Corrective Services. In many ways, Schneidas's case became the focus of a battle between the prison authorities trying to reform the system and the prison officers trying to maintain the old ways.

Schneidas's letters from this time express a remarkable shift in outlook, as if he had been given a new lease on life. He seemed determined to rehabilitate himself and, for the first time, to confront his emotions:

> I'll be able to start rebuilding my life. We do a lot of group work in this unit. The whole thing is based on a type of group therapy. It's forcing me to look at aspects of myself that I'd wanted to keep locked away, that I didn't want to confront. It's funny how you can keep kidding yourself for years without really being aware of it. I suppose I've just come to a stage of my life and in my circumstances where I have to stop playing games with myself. It's a new experience.

The 'truth in sentencing' legislation was introduced in New South Wales in 1990, affecting all inmates serving a life sentence at that time. Previously, 'life' was an arbitrary sentence (at Her Majesty's pleasure). Since 1990, inmates receiving life sentences are imprisoned for the term of their natural life. Schneidas's sentence was redetermined and a non-parole period, or release date, was set. In handing down this decision, Justice Grove noted that he:

> ... could not help notice that the applicant has a custom of subscribing correspondence 'yours hopefully' followed by his signature ... I do not have jurisdiction to order actual release, but I would commend to those responsible for this, the observation that the applicant's virtual lifetime in institutional custody of one kind or another means that it will never be known if the applicant can adjust to community life until he is given the opportunity to try.[5]

Schneidas found out about life on the outside a few years ago, when he was released to begin a new life with his wife in Sydney's south. I spoke to him by phone a few months after his release and asked if he would take part in a book I was writing about the lives and religious outlook of members of Sydney's Jewish community. I assumed he would turn me down, but he readily agreed, and when I asked why he had done so, he responded with a question of his own. 'Do you know what a *drek* is?' he asked. I answered yes, knowing it to be a Yiddish word for lowly, scum, dirt-like. He continued: 'Without God, I am *drek*'.

On the morning of the interview, the phone rang just as I was walking out the door; it was Schneidas calling to cancel our meeting. He was apologetic and sounded distraught, saying there were too many things for him to sort out in his life. A few weeks later he was found dead in a south coast retreat.

The more I learnt of Schneidas's experiences the more I was convinced that his life became a tragedy which could have been averted. There seemed to be so many opportunities for appropriate intervention that may have seen an outcome other than the murder of prison officer Mewburn and the waste of Schneidas's life. I began to wonder: did the system entrusted to punish and rehabilitate him actually play a role in creating the violent criminal he became?

Of all the documents I came across relating to his case, none affected me more than a submission to the NSW Minister for Corrective Services on Schneidas's behalf by prison counsellor Robert Hockley, who visited him during his hunger strike:

> He was intelligent, challenging, aggressive, manipulative and very impatient. One day, after about eight months, he was telling me about an incident in his childhood which hinted at his loneliness and fear. After I responded to this he revealed a profound feeling of hopelessness. His eyes filled and he backed away from the trapdoor. He changed the subject, but it was too late. He had shared a part of himself he hardly knew. We had made contact. I had met the boy in the man.
>
> I will grieve for Schneidas if he must die now. My sadness will be for the little boy whose broken family, emotional deprivation and migrant status led to the state boys' home and then to the prison system. From the age of nine he has been consistently exposed to the violence and brutality inherent in these systems. Schneidas is therefore a tragic figure, with no alternative but to develop a tough protective shell around the vulnerable self and violent ways of resolving conflict, in order to survive.[6]

Schneidas's experience profoundly affected me. I wanted to know if anything had changed since he first entered prison. I knew the reception biff no longer existed but was curious to learn whether prison is still such an inhumane place. I wanted to know whether there were any commonalities among people sentenced to prison and if their backgrounds offered any clues. What is it like to live in prison? What impact does incarceration have on inmates? And, most importantly, what kind of people do criminals turn out to be upon their release into society?

Armed with these questions, and following many months of preparation, I received permission to enter the Long Bay Prison complex to interview inmates, and I continued doing so every two or three weeks for the next two-and-a-half years. The result is this account of prison life, told in the words of serving inmates.

Welcome to a society that you will hopefully never have cause to experience first-hand, but nevertheless should be familiar with.

Introduction

Equipped with a note on departmental letterhead authorising me to meet with inmates, I then had to find some. My intention was to meet with each prisoner four times: the first time, without recording equipment, to introduce myself and build a rapport. The second time, this time with recording equipment, to find out about their family background and childhood; the third time to focus on their later youth, up to their current incarceration; and the fourth time to hear their experiences of prison and their plans for the future. I planned to speak to as many inmates as necessary until I felt I had learnt enough to tell their individual stories and offer collective insights.

In preparation for these visits, I devoured every book I could find based on inmates' own words, in Australia and overseas. Chief among them were several of Tony Parker's books based on inmate conversations spanning several decades in the United Kingdom and the United States.[7] Parker applied one major criterion above all when selecting inmates, which I took up early on: the inmates must take responsibility for their crime. Otherwise, invariably, the conversation would focus on alleged miscarriages of justice. This stipulation was also out of respect for the victims of the crimes, who did not need a reminder of their pain, particularly in the form of a denial from the person found by the courts to be responsible. The New South Wales Department of Corrective Services made this same request of me. Surprisingly, perhaps, it was the only request made. Otherwise, I was not censored in any way and my conversations with the inmates were conducted in private.

All I had to do next was send Bob Stapleton, a veteran of the department's public relations office, a fax describing the type of inmate I wanted to interview. Guided by a quasi-quantitative approach, I set down the various permutations of the prison population including age, ethnicity, geographical location, type of crime committed and duration and stage of sentence. I succeeded in covering some of these more than others.

The specifications would typically read something like: 'Violent crime, lengthy sentence and having served most of it'. Bob would then send these specifications on to the governors of several prisons through departmental mail. The governors, in turn, would circulate the request among inmates they deemed appropriate or thought would be willing to be interviewed.

The individual governors ultimately had final say over my entry into their prisons. As expected, some governors turned out to be very helpful and others not, and I realised that some facilities were going to be accommodating while others would prove elusive. One interview that was deemed too controversial and denied to me was with a transsexual inmate who had served time in both men's and women's prisons.

I limited my requests to prisons within the Sydney area, as I was also holding down a full-time job that, although flexible, did require my ongoing presence. Long Bay, consisting of five prisons within one complex and only a twenty-minute drive from the CBD, was my best option, particularly as it housed the maximum-security Violence Prevention Program (VPP). The other was Silverwater, which mainly houses inmates awaiting trial or sentencing and those in protective custody.

Several weeks later, Bob Stapleton phoned to let me know that he had found the first inmate who had agreed to speak to me, and we set a time to meet with Jason. Bob would accompany me on the initial visit—probably to reassure the department of my intentions—then leave me alone with the inmates for subsequent interviews.

Early in my research I decided to concentrate solely on male prisoners. Women make up a relatively small proportion of the prison population, with just under 600 incarcerated state-wide, although their numbers are increasing at a staggering rate[8]—in the seven years to 2002, the proportion of female inmates in Australian prisons rose from 4.9 per cent to 6.6 per cent of the prison population.[9] My reasoning was that the issues affecting women in prison are very different to those affecting men, and I felt that attempting to cover both in one book would be too ambitious to do either well.

I had intended to include interviews with prison officers and other staff members to gain their perspective, and went as far as interviewing a few before abandoning the idea. Having spoken to the first, whose manner was frank and stories were fascinating, I realised I would not receive his authorisation to publish the interview. It was too unrealistic to expect those who work within the prison system to openly criticise their workplace and the result would be unbalanced. They also could not discuss things that take place within prisons that are not supposed to, such as incidents of staff smuggling contraband into prisons either for financial gain or due to blackmail.

I found the majority of prison officers I came across to be friendly, interested in my work and helpful. A few, as expected, were less than happy to see me, and on the rare occasion I came across officers who resented my presence.

Inmates by and large treated me with apathy, curiosity or friendliness. When I entered the VPP I participated in the inmates' weekly show-and-tell session, where selected inmates would play a song or display a painting or other item they used to express themselves. I would introduce myself and explain why I was there. Once I had been spotted around the prison wing a few times, familiar faces would nod to me but I never really knew how the inmates viewed my presence.

The wide road, open space and ocean glimpses that lead to the Long Bay Prison complex seem out of context—it is a deceptively serene drive, particularly on a brilliant Sydney morning. One bend of the road, however, and the tranquillity is gone, displaced by the imposing stone walls of the prison complex, which appear without warning.

Long Bay is infamous in Sydney. It is a place everyone hears of from time to time in the news but few people visit. Yet the public is curious. A morbid fascination abounds about prison life and particularly about prison violence. This fascination is encouraged by the popular media and even creates unlikely and somewhat macabre identities such as Mark 'Chopper' Read.

In Australia, as in the United States, the prison population has grown at a phenomenal rate. The United States currently incarcerates over two million people, making its correctional institutions the twenty-second most populous state in the country. Another way of putting it is that at any time, one in every thirty-two adults in the United States is either on probation, serving time or on parole. Even more staggering is the fact that, on average, 12 per cent of African-Americans in their twenties and early thirties are currently in jail.[10] In New South Wales, the last inmate census, con-ducted in 2001, showed that the state had, on average, 7667 inmates in full-time custody, up from 6372 four years earlier, and 17 000 people on parole or probation.[11] The Department of Corrective Services anticipates there will be 9000 prison inmates in New South Wales by 2005.[12]

Contrary to popular perceptions this growth is not related to an increase in violent crime. The public, fuelled by a media that knows how well fear sells, believes that Sydney is an increasingly dangerous place to live. This is despite the fact that violent crime in Australia, and indeed in most Western countries, has remained relatively stable for the past three decades and is lower than it was a hundred years ago.[13] What we have seen, rather, is a phenomenal increase in drug-related arrests and drug-related crimes, which now account for 80 per cent of inmates.[14] More than half of the inmates entering prison report suffering from a drug- or alcohol-related problem and 80 per cent reported having suffered from one at some point in their life.[15]

There is a vicious cycle at play here: media outlets sensationalise stories and the public becomes fearful, demanding more policing and lengthier sentences from politicians, who respond by setting tougher sentencing guidelines, stricter bail rules and putting additional police on the streets, leading to more arrests. And so our prison population increases.

Having put more people in prison, for longer periods of time, the question remains: what happens next?

When researching this book, I wanted to consider how well our prison system achieves its goals. It does accomplish some of its aims, but I wanted to know how the system fared at what I consider to be the most challenging one of all—the rehabilitation of its inmates into productive members of society, or at least less destructive ones.

Prison succeeds in punishing criminals. As will become evident in the following chapters, prison is an unpleasant environment that deprives inmates of their liberty and dictates their daily regime. Prison also succeeds at isolating those who commit crime from the rest of society, ensuring that for the duration of their sentence inmates will not be able to harm the public. The jury is out on just how successfully prison acts as a deterrent to others and whether longer sentences in harsher conditions make any difference in this respect.

The question of deterrence is most often applied to debates about the death penalty, which is used in many American states. While serving as the governor of Texas, George W Bush executed 152 inmates, more than any other governor in United States history.[16] In answer to a journalist's question, Bush said that if the death penalty were proven to be an ineffective deterrent he would no longer support the practice, 'I don't think you should support the death penalty to seek revenge, I don't think that's right. I think the reason to support the death penalty is because it saves other people's lives.'[17] We know, however, that crime levels bear no relation to sentences—in the United States, states that do not impose the death penalty experience less murders than those that do.[18] In a 1988 report (updated in 2000), the United Nations concluded that 'it is not prudent to accept the hypothesis that capital punishment deters murder to a greater extent than does the threat and application of the supposedly lesser punishment of life imprisonment'.[19]

This leaves one more goal for the prison system, the most difficult one to accomplish: the rehabilitation of inmates and thus the creation of a safer society. But the public, angry at having its sense of security compromised, wants the perpetrators of crimes to be made to pay by being incarcerated in as unpleasant conditions as humanely acceptable. This gives rise to the central question this book sets out to explore: can the state rehabilitate and punish a person simultaneously?

In the following chapters, you will hear from seven inmates about the reality of Australian prison life. You will learn that our prison system suffers from a revolving door syndrome and often creates poorly adjusted, angrier people who are likely to commit further crimes and serve more time in prison.

Most often I would meet with the inmates early or mid morning, which seemed to be when they were free from activities. I would park in the public car park and walk through Long Bay's sprawling grounds; the well-manicured lawns looked after by free-roaming low-security inmates. It was not uncommon for me to be turned away at the main gate—if there had been a disturbance by inmates the previous night or industrial action by officers, the prison would go into lock-down mode, meaning that all inmates were restricted to their cells and could not receive visitors. (I was told that this once occurred so officers could watch the Olympic torch relay pass the prison.)

Once I made it past the main boom gate, I would climb the hill towards the imposing metal gate leading into Long Bay's Malabar Special Programs Centre.

The building, which houses maximum-security inmates, was imposing, and to enter it meant negotiating several prison gates. The first was a solid stone wall built when the jail first opened in the early nineteenth century, and was modelled on older style English prisons like that seen in the English comedy *Porridge*. Solid metal gates appear in the wall at intervals, each leading to a different part of the centre. Standing before a metal door with a small window at eye level, I buzzed the intercom and then entered a holding yard, which was large enough to fit a small truck. A prison officer checked my paperwork, pointed me to the sign-in book, and placed a call into the prison. (He also advised me to leave my mobile phone behind—these are especially powerful devices in prison where inmates can only dial a selection of pre-approved numbers and their calls are monitored. As mobile phones decrease in size, they are easier to smuggle and hide, and the problem is exacerbated.)

In the holding area I waited to be escorted into the prison wing proper, through the asphalt yard. Once my officer escort emerged from behind yet another metal gate, I was allowed through. Two more doors and a labyrinth of corridors later I reached the officers' station, where several were seated overlooking black-and-white monitors that provided constant surveillance of the wing. On the wall were numbered slots with a card displaying each inmate's cell number and particulars.

The relevant inmate was then sought out by an officer or their name was announced over the loudspeaker. The officers then began their search for an undisturbed room to conduct the interview in, a different location each time. On clement days we sometimes sat outside in a locked yard; other times we conducted the interview in empty rooms, cells and common rooms—once even in the governor's office on his day off.

Only once—on my way out of the maximum-security unit when the officers were out of earshot—did two inmates (not the inmates I was interviewing) ask me for a favour. Both had girlfriends at Mulawa Women's Prison and asked that I pass on some letters for them. Both showed clear displeasure at my refusal. The inmates I interviewed did not ask me for anything, nor were they ever threatening or aggressive. Partly this reflected the nature of the inmates who agreed to be interviewed and the prisons I went to. Mostly, I think, the inmates enjoyed having someone take a genuine interest in their lives.

People often ask whether I was frightened while inside the prisons. I was apprehensive on my first visit, but the reception I received from the inmates and staff was relaxed enough for my fear to quickly dissipate. (There was, however, one exception. I had just completed an interview inside a cell in the maximum-security wing. We said our goodbyes and the inmate left, leaving me to make my own way to the gate leading to the outside world. Having been seen by the officer on the other side, I stood at the door for what seemed a long time. Eventually I knocked and said, 'I'd like to leave now', to which she replied, 'Don't you all'. In the seconds it took to clarify the confusion I did entertain the idea of remaining locked up due to a red-tape tangle.)

When a quiet space was found and we were alone, the inmate and I would chat for a while about nothing in par-ticular. On second and subsequent visits I brought out my tape recorder, pad of paper and pen. I explained that I would be relying on their words for this book and that nothing they said would be published without their written consent. I explained that occasionally I would jot down something that came to mind that I wanted to ask about later. Then the interviews began.

What follows is my understanding of prison based on my in-depth conversations with seven inmates. Interspersed with my own observations, what you are about to read is what I was told verbatim. The words I attribute to individual inmates are indeed their own and remain unchanged, other than some grammatical corrections. I hope this will allow readers to draw their own conclusions.

Welcome to prison.

Chapter 1:

Meet the Inmates

The prospect of embarking on my first inmate interview, especially knowing it would be a long time before I finished the last, was made less daunting by my working life. By profession I am a social researcher, with much of my time spent in focus groups and in-depth interviews listening to Australians of all ages talk about aspects of their lives. I have learnt to treat each interview as unique and inspiring— as people's lives are. Everyone has a story to tell, and those who insist they do not usually have the most interesting ones. The challenge is to encourage people to express themselves openly while being careful not to probe issues that are too sensitive or raw, or that once broached could not be resolved adequately in the two hours of an interview (and in any event, could not be resolved by me).

In my toolbox were several insights I employ in every interview: that silence can be the best input from an interviewer, that people do not always say what they mean, and that what people choose not to say can be as significant as what they do say.

Causing some concern, however, were the forewarnings I had read of the particular challenges prison inmates may pose as interviewees. Inmates, for example, are naturally mistrustful of officials, outsiders or anyone asking them too many questions. Even more problematic was the likelihood of being taken for a ride. Inmates' lives are greatly restricted and they are preoccupied with finding ways of beating the system, ridiculing it, rising above it. With nothing to gain from speaking with me, there was a chance that what I would hear would not be the whole truth.

These concerns, as far as I could tell, did not materialise. However naive, I felt that what I was told was truthful and I did connect with the inmates on some level and build a rapport with them. This is something readers will ultimately have to judge for themselves.

On my side I had basic human nature. We all yearn to be listened to, for our stories to be heard by others, and I offered inmates a genuine and attentive audience. I shared with them my purpose in wishing to hear their stories and, once they had spoken with me for a while, the inmates seemed to accept this at face value. Of equal significance perhaps, I also offered them a public forum for their prison experiences and the chance to see their own words in print.

The prison telegraph is an efficient one and word of my presence quickly got around. After a while, particularly once I became a familiar face around the VPP, inmates would ask me to hear their stories too, and there was no shortage of volunteers.

The words the inmates used in telling their stories are raw and sometimes inarticulate. Some of the incidents they describe, in which pain is inflicted and suffered, may be uncomfortable to read. These also remain unchanged.

Jason

It was 9.30 on a Thursday morning when I met up with Bob Stapleton, a veteran of the Department of Corrective Services' public relations office, outside the main gate at the base of the Long Bay Prison complex, my car one of only a handful in the adjoining car park. I hopped into his car and with a wave from the guard we drove through, took a right turn and parked across the lawn from the minimum-security prison where Jason was expecting us.

Having made our presence known to the governor, Bob and I were shown to a small room just outside the main building that houses the inmates; it was bare except for two chairs and a white formica table. It was not long before Jason walked in. Aged twenty-nine, tall and thin, he was wearing a green long-sleeved shirt buttoned up to the collar.

In prison one finds every shade of green, being the official colour of inmate attire (with the exception of running shoes, which tend to be popular brands). While the prison officers, whose designated colour is blue, wear uniforms, inmates can mix and match any clothing—as long as it is green. I made sure not to wear blue, for obvious reasons, and seeing as I own nothing in green, maintained a neutral fashion presence throughout my visits.

I knew little about Jason other than that he was serving a sentence for manslaughter and was well into his sentence. This being my first interview, Jason's shyness and quiet voice eased my nerves. He was so softly spoken that occasionally I had to ask him to speak up. I explained the purpose of my visit, and during the next hour and a half we spent together, I learnt that he was approaching his first parole hearing, having served the minimum part of his sentence. This would either see him walk out the gates soon after or stay put for a further six months before being able to apply again. He was optimistic, more so than Bob when I asked him on our drive back to the car park what Jason's chances were. 'They don't usually give it to long-termers the first time', he told me. 'They usually want to give them a chance to do some programs like work release first.'

A week later, Jason greeted me at our second meeting. This time he was wearing a T-shirt, his bare arms—previously concealed from sight—revealing a tapestry of tattoos extending down to his wrists. Had I passed him in the streets as I saw him the previous week, he would not have made a particular impression on me, but this time his appearance was strikingly more intimidating—until he began speaking, that is. Once the tape was switched on and our chat began, he seemed to relax and the conversation became fluent.

With Jason's permission, between visits I looked up the transcript of the judgment and sentence from his court case. Following is, in part, what the judge had to say:

> Whilst the deceased was on the lounge watching the television the accused went into the kitchen where he took a sharp pointed kitchen knife with a blade of about six inches. He returned and stabbed the deceased ... He said the deceased stood up and said to him, 'what are you doing, man?' but the accused, speaking of himself, said, 'I couldn't stop'. The deceased went into the bathroom where the accused said he stabbed him twice more. The deceased then went into the hallway by the front door where he sank to the floor and the accused stabbed him again.
>
> ... I have come to the view that the appropriate overall sentence to impose is that of penal servitude for a period of fourteen years, comprising a minimum period of nine years and an additional term of five years.[20]

Jason was likeable and easy to interview. Of all the inmates, he seemed the least suspicious of me and spoke the most openly; it was as if he already had one foot on the outside. He told me that the desire to tell his story was motivated by his newfound devotion to Christianity and the aim of helping others avoid making the mistakes he did.

Shane

I was not surprised to discover that Shane had been in the navy for several years; everything about him and the space surrounding him was perfectly neat and ordered. In his late thirties and with short-cropped hair, he was also meticulously polite, offering a cup of coffee and seat immediately upon my arrival, with a wide smile and firm shake of the hand.

Shane was my introduction to the maximum-security Violence Prevention Program (VPP), housed in the Alexander Maconochie Unit at Long Bay, where I conducted the rest of my interviews. Here inmates with a history of violent crimes, who apply and are deemed appropriate, spend several months intensively examining the source of their violence in order to learn more appropriate reactions to situations. The program aims to encourage inmates not to revert to criminal and violent behaviour when released into society by making them confront their violent tendencies and their origins.

Shane was not a participant of the VPP; he was in fact disqualified from most prison programs due to his 'E' classification, representing escapee. (In court it was alleged that while working in the prison garage, he donned an officer's uniform and drove out the main gate in an officer's car.) Rather, he was the chef in the wing, which is renowned among inmates for its excellent food. The variety and quality of food take on special meaning in prison, where there is little else to mark the passage of time, and the standard of food varies greatly from one facility to the next. Several inmates told me that the food, along with the less tense environment, was enough reason for some to apply to participate in the VPP.

Shane's accommodation at the time of our interviews would have been the envy of any inmate. With inmates only occupying the main two-storey wing, the smaller wing, situated behind the officers' station and normally housing twenty inmates, was empty except for Shane and his kitchen hand. With a pool table, kitchenette and coffee table surrounded by cushioned seats, the area looked more like a student union lounge than a prison.

Once locked inside the unit, we sat in the lounge area. On other occasions, when the weather permitted, Shane asked the officers to open the gate at the end of the wing and we sat outside under a blue sky, broken by high brick walls and razor wire.

Solidly built, Shane is adorned with large tattoos (carefully positioned to be concealed by clothing) on his torso, back and upper arms. Shane has been in and out of jail his entire adult life and at the time of our interviews was serving a sentence for sixty armed robbery convictions, many of which he told me he was appealing. He was convinced, however, that his days of drug addiction and armed robbery were over for good. He showed no outward signs of institutionalisation. Like Jason, he seemed genuinely appreciative of the opportunity to share his story and future plans, as if affirming these to himself by saying them aloud. At one stage I pointed out to him that his mild manner and friendly disposition did not fit my preconceived image of an inmate, especially a violent one. He concurred, offering the following story:

I went to a school reunion just after I completed my first jail sentence. People were saying to me 'Shane, we thought you'd be the last person to go to jail', and so did I. It was just inconceivable. I had people say to me, 'Shane, you had a career, you're in the navy, you had so much going for you, then you went to jail. What the hell happened?' Well, shit does happen, and that's the way things pan out.

David

David was the first Aboriginal Australian inmate who agreed to speak with me, and the more of his story he relayed the more surprised I was by his readiness to tell it. I found inmates to be suspicious by nature, especially Indigenous inmates such as David, who feel disenfranchised from and essentially at war with white society. When I asked David how the other Aboriginal inmates felt about him speaking to me, he said that word of my presence had passed around after I began interviewing Jason. Based on David's wish to do something to help break the cycle of violence, the elders within the prison, to whom David deferred for approval, agreed.

I had read and heard a lot about the dysfunctional existence of many Aboriginal Australians—how they live with a prevailing sense of displacement on the fringes of society—but I had never had the opportunity to hear their experiences first-hand and in such depth.

Prior to my research for this book, I was also aware that prison is a violent place, but I did not know how much of what I had read, or seen in movies, reflected reality. I was uncertain whether any of the inmates would discuss experiences of violence, be they victim or perpetrator, but David was candid and forthcoming when recounting experiences as a perpetrator of violence. He openly admitted responsibility for countless acts of senseless aggression and the humiliation and subjugation of countless victims. He decided to join the VPP after he began having nightmares about the torture he had inflicted on others.

Despite the fact that David kept his eyes fixed on my own much of the time, he was somewhat detached, as if his mind was in a faraway place. Looking younger than his early thirties, he exuded calm and confidence.

I found it disconcerting to become as relaxed as I did in David's company; in different circumstances I may have found him menacing—he is in jail for taking part in the random bashing and killing of a man, purely because he was believed to be gay. Throughout our conversations I felt unsure how to respond to David's accounts of extreme cruelty and his revelry in the suffering of others. He alternated between serious, remorseful insights and sporadic laughter when reminded of an episode and its helpless victim:

> If you see a bloke crying over the phone, well he's a target, you can do things to him and no-one else is going to know about it. Except out here you've got the baddest people: your killers, your rapists; you've got everybody. You've got to be very careful what you do because you can piss off the wrong person. You've got your gangs and if you're not in a clique you're going to cop it from all ends. It's hard, very hard, when you don't know no-one.

David's mother was part of the stolen generations, and was forcibly removed from her parents and community as a child.

This was a fate David assumed could befall him at any time throughout his childhood, and a sense of disenfranchisement is a feature of his story. When I asked about his beliefs, he answered, 'I believe in dreamtime. I don't believe in heaven. I believe we live in hell and the place we go is the dreamtime, back to our totems'.

Michael

While he identifies as Aboriginal Australian, Michael's background is complex.

> *My grandfather on my mum's side was a black South African and my grandfather's father was a black South African, my grandmother's mother was a white South African.*

Michael's pale skin easily passes him as Caucasian and allows him to blend into both cultures.

> *With me, a lot of people didn't know that I was Aboriginal. I didn't care that my friends were white because my dad was white too.*

Michael's family background is an example of extreme dysfunctionality. His father was a violent alcoholic and his mother gave birth to him at sixteen—the same age that Michael too became a father—and she was often unable to look after him while dealing with her own addiction to heroin. Michael spent his childhood being shuffled between various relatives who could care for him, but he felt no sense of belonging or safety. Consequently he sought and found belonging among his friends, and together they carved a path of destruction revolving around drugs, alcohol and crime.

In some ways, rather than absorbing both white and Aboriginal culture, Michael appears lost within both. In the one sentence he says, 'I believe in God and in the Lord Jesus Christ', followed by 'I want to know but I don't know about Arnhem land and the full bloods really, what their beliefs are.'

Interestingly, despite or perhaps because of his unsettled life, Michael has remained committed to the same woman for well over a decade. No longer addicted to drugs, he comes across as a much gentler person than his record of violence attests to, and claims to have made a commitment that this will be his last term in prison. Michael described his motivations for ending a life of crime and drugs:

> For me, it was my children, my wife and myself. They wanted me to change a long time before I actually did. My daughter will be eleven when I get out and I was eleven when my father came and picked me up, and all I can see is that I've inflicted my whole life on her through my behaviour, my actions. And had I had that time again that would never happen. At the time maybe I didn't know what I should have known and I can't change time. All I can do is make the most of what's left.

Stuart

Short and in his mid to late forties, Stuart was a likeable character with a kind face. It was easy being in his company and my conversations with him were, perhaps, the most fluent of all, with my questions and his stories flowing seamlessly. In one interview I told him that it was hard to imagine him as violent, for he did not appear at all threatening. I asked if he considered himself violent still. 'It is there,' he answered, 'it's there. I've learnt to control it now. I don't know what it is. I used to have raged thoughts and if I acted on them ... there's no amount of things I could have done. No-one could stop me.'

Stuart was keen to share his experiences with me, almost treating our meetings as part of his rehabilitation. The VPP had forced him to examine himself for the first time in his life and seemed to have offered an impetus for change. 'I had a lot of pain, but hidden pain', he told me. 'I used to hide it. Pain that I couldn't solve, things I couldn't solve. I wanted to get to the basis of why that rage was there.'

He was serving a sentence for manslaughter, having killed a former neighbour in an altercation involving a kitchen knife:

> I had an act of rage, okay, and a guy dies, okay? Now I have to look at myself for my own benefit because I don't want to do it again. This is why I came to the program, to give me some sort of feedback so that I can deal with society again and be put into a situation and be able to deal with it in a way where it doesn't cause problems. And that whole build-up to that point of my crime was all my life just dealing with it in short spurts and not having a real good look at myself. So it's amazing you have to come to jail to find something.

As an inmate, Stuart had turned a corner and had stopped fighting the system:

I looked upon using the incarceration period as a learning point for me because I don't want to make a mistake in life again. I mean I will make mistakes but I don't want to make a big giant one like that, where it just takes you away from society and puts you in this environment.

I do not know how well Stuart faired in the general prison population, and he was reluctant to speak of any personal experiences of violence. Several weeks after our final interview, I saw Stuart while I was taking a tour of Wing Ten, a maximum-security facility nearby that has an atmosphere considerably tenser then the VPP. There was a hive of activity as inmates played card games, visited each other's cells and milled around the wing. I roamed freely for several minutes, trying to disguise my discomfort. The wing housed several inmates participating in an art course, one of whom gave me a tour of his prize-winning artwork that decorated his cell. From there I paused at a card table surrounded by four intense-looking middle-aged men who urged me to move on in a most succinct and convincing way with a 'fuck off'. On my way out, I saw Stuart at a distance and instinctively waved to him, perhaps too enthusiastically for his wellbeing.

Gordon

Gordon holds the honour of being arguably the state's most accomplished bank robber, but perhaps not that successful considering he has spent all but six months since 1979 in prison. Gordon was well into his forties and was the oldest and longest-serving of the inmates I spoke with. Sometimes he spoke in a murmur and occasionally I found it difficult to understand him. He also appeared quite detached during our conversations—I never felt he trusted or wished to connect with me.

Gordon said that he agreed to speak with me because he was tired of crime and prison and that he was ready to call it a day. Speaking with me was a public expression of his retirement from crime once the four years left on his sentence expire.

We first met in an unoccupied cell, one of a row lining the walls of the ground floor of the main wing in the VPP. For reasons unknown to Gordon or me, during the first of our interviews a prison officer sat beside the cell door, just out of earshot. Few inmates roamed the floor; most were either in a group or individual therapy program or outside in the yard playing handball or smoking.

Gordon's facial features showed the scars of many battles over the years. The ever-present violence throughout his life was as astonishing to me as my lack of violent experiences was to him:

> *Someone's come up to me and said they've never had a fight in their life. Like Jason here, he's a psychologist; he's told me he's never had a fight in his life. Well, I find that hard to believe, I just can't. Well, I can now, but at the time I couldn't fathom it. We're living in two different worlds. It's just hard for me to comprehend that you've never had a fight in your life. That was my lifestyle, you know?*

During the course of our interviews Gordon was somewhat of a minor celebrity, with *60 Minutes* interviewing him for a story on how banks can secure themselves against robberies. Only twice did I momentarily note a softer side to Gordon: he revealed slight nervousness before the filming of the *60 Minutes* story, and pride—or prison celebrity perhaps—after it aired.

Darren

Tall, lanky and in his mid to late twenties, Darren was the most animated and highly emotive of the inmates I spoke with. He was also the most unsettling to interview. Take, for example, his macabre fascination with murder and murderers that he shared with me one morning:

> *I like murder and I like serial killers and I like Stephen King, just really gory books. And I've thought if I'm capable of some of these gruesome crimes. I could do it most certainly, but would I? Would anything turn me or make me that mad to do it? I don't think so. Maybe if you hurt my mother there wouldn't be a hesitation. But other than that, it's not my go.*
>
> *I've started collecting clippings of those I admire. I don't intend to go out there and deadset cut people up or anything but it fascinates me how brilliant people like Jeffrey Dahmer are. How did they become so evil when they're so highly respected in the community? What made them twist? That's what I'm interested in; I find it very fascinating.*

Darren described how he is drawn to what he believes to be the immortality achieved by celebrated murderers:

> *It's like Adolf Hitler. I really do admire the bloke because he went out and took the initiative and done*

what he did but he also got defeated. He most certainly hurt people. It's war. He done what he did, what he had to, and he made a deadset name for himself. He will never ever die, ever. He basically lives. He will be known two hundred years from now.

I like Martin Bryant too, but I don't like what he did to the kids. I don't mind people who kill adults, I really don't, because adults can be replaced by younger siblings [children], you know. He just had a bad day, he had enough, he snapped. He could've been one of the nicest blokes around but something ticked him off. Could've [been] he didn't have enough for a Mars bar, anything, who knows? But he did what he had to do.

Although friendly, respectful towards me and occasionally apologetic for the pain he had caused others, at other times Darren was oblivious to the magnitude of his crimes:

I know a bloke who's been in two or three times for murders and that, and he's a beautiful man, very intelligent, very soft spoken and very kind. Had a bad day. That is all. So, I can't blame him for that, we all go through it, but some express it a little more harshly than others.

In his own words, Darren was destined for prison— he described it as if it were a designated career path; his ambition:

I wanted to do ten years' jail. Most of my friends were in jail and I said that before I finish my career I want to do at least ten years. I've done nearly nine so maybe if they don't give me my parole I'll do ten, and that will be it. I think that I can put it to rest because I really don't want to do any more time.

When I asked Darren about his plans for when the gates opened and he walked through the prison car park a free man, he responded:

I might go into town for a day or so. Automatically, I think, I'll be searching as well, like not meaning to but I'll be doing it. It's not as if I'm intending to do something but I will be looking, most certainly. There's a chance I'll do something, most certainly. If I get down and out or bored, why not?

My ideal of doing things is robbing people and I can't see anything beyond that or around it. I don't want to dress up and go to a restaurant or meet people and go ... to ... clubs. I don't want to do that shit. I need adrenaline. I don't do it by jumping off a bridge or going down a cliff or something, but inflicting, not so much pain but afflicting fear into people. That's what I like to do and that's it.

Darren was released not long after our final interview and was returned to jail shortly after.

Chapter 2:
A Bad Start

By my second visit, each inmate had had some time to decide whether they were prepared to go ahead with the interviews and, if so, what they wanted to talk about. Once the inmate and I had settled into a private space and chatted for a while about nothing in particular, I would place my cassette recorder on the table or chair between us and press the record button. I would then begin by asking the inmate to describe his background, family and childhood.

My style of questioning was largely open-ended, allowing the inmates to emphasise whichever part of their story they felt was important. My task was to listen attentively and respond appropriately, offering a new question or clarifying something they had just said. I had no qualms in declaring my ignorance and asking them to slow down or explain prison jargon—I was there to learn from them, and told them so.

I shared with the inmates my assessment that prison is something people hear about in the media, are innately interested in, but in actual fact know little about and that this was an opportunity for them to let the public know what life in jail is really like.

Some inmates showed signs of nervousness at first, but this dissipated once they had talked for several minutes, and our time together usually passed quickly.

The inmates' backgrounds and childhoods seemed a good place to start, and I was curious to learn whether there were common threads in their upbringings that shaped their lives. Was there was a pattern to their experiences? Do the majority of violent people originate from a violent environment?

The answer, I learnt very early on, was an unequivocal yes. Each inmate in turn offered a story of a sad childhood in a dysfunctional home where nurturing and expressions of emotions were largely absent. All experienced violence regularly and learnt early on that aggression was an appropriate outlet for frustration, disappointment and a myriad of other emotions. They also learnt that violence was a legitimate expression of masculinity. A pattern emerged of a link between the perpetrators of violence and a violent upbringing. Violence was instilled in these inmates from a young age and guided them from their earliest memories.

It quickly became clear that the inmates do not hold their mothers responsible for the direction their lives have taken. It was fascinating to listen to these hardened men speak of their mothers with tenderness and devotion—this was especially so among the Indigenous inmates. And although this reverence was not always manifested in their behaviour towards their mothers, they were relationships fraught with guilt and deep affection.

The inmates did acknowledge their mothers' shortcomings. However, they also appreciated that their mothers, who at the time were faced with their own emotional problems and limitations, loved and provided for them to the best of their abilities under the circumstances.

When I asked about their fathers, however, the tone of the conversations became far more reflective. It was interesting that the inmates commonly began by praising their fathers, as if defending them against allegations I had not made. With gentle probing I encouraged them to express their real feelings, something the inmates in the VPP were learning that it was okay to do—that their pent-up feelings were legitimate, and airing them was a positive step.

The conversations about their fathers evoked the most emotional responses from the inmates; their voices sometimes wavered and their answers were interspersed with long pauses and what appeared to be painful recollections. At times they became distant as they pondered unreconciled emotions.

The fathers described by the inmates were men for whom masculinity was defined through traditional macho stereotypes. They were hard men who were impossible to please and who seldom, if ever, provided warmth or reassurance for their children. Most profoundly, perhaps, they instilled constant fear in their children and reinforced this with fists, belts and whips. Through programs such as the VPP, the inmates began to recognise that the abuse they received had more to do with their fathers' extreme moods or drunken states than anything they may have done to warrant punishment.

Jason grew up in a country town that had a population of 12 000 people. He described his family as dysfunctional and believed that such a childhood environment is common among prison inmates.

JASON: I suppose my childhood was all right; my parents always gave us everything we needed physically ... they just didn't know how to give us what we needed emotionally. I never got much love and attention so I went towards the negative [way] of thinking.

One thing I would say about the majority of people in jail is that they are from dysfunctional families, brought up in very emotionless families. My father was a man's man, and I think that was the era when a lot of men were like that. I believe it's an emotional weakness.

Shane also grew up in the country, where his distant and disciplinarian father exacerbated his sense of isolation.

SHANE: In my childhood there wasn't a lot of love, we never kissed or cuddled. I don't know whether that was because we weren't loved or if that's just the way they were. It was a dysfunctional family in the sense that our family wasn't a unit. Dad was in Sydney Monday to Friday so I only seen him thirty-six hours a week, and he would demand of me to make sure things were done and if I didn't do this and didn't do that then I'd get a strapping. I've always been judged for the bad things I've done in my life, not the good things.

Shane—along with his siblings—was adopted at birth, a fact he learnt unexpectedly.

SHANE: One day they went to a concert or something, and my sister said, 'You know, Mum and Dad aren't our real mum and dad'. I was a bit stunned, as you could probably well imagine. I have never really sat down ... and discussed my adoption with my parents; it's something they don't really wish to speak about.

The desire for paternal approval was a hope the inmates found difficult to relinquish; some still longed for it. This hope motivated Shane throughout his childhood and teenage years. He related his unenthusiastic enlistment in the Royal Australian Navy and the ensuing disappointment.

SHANE: I always had my mind set on being a mechanic after I finished year ten and my parents thought that the best way to obtain the qualification was [in] the defence forces. I was fifteen years old and really wasn't keen on doing that, but I felt that I had to do what my parents wanted me to do. It's a big call to adopt children and to … raise them, but I can't understand why two people would adopt five children and when they got to a certain age force them to leave home and put them into careers whether they liked to or not. That's basically how it was with all of us.

When I was selected to go [in] to the navy, that was a pretty proud moment in my life because they only took sixty people out of six hundred. I went to Western Australia to do my training. I missed my family, I missed being on the farm, I was so far away from anybody it wasn't funny. I was homesick, I was young, I had no love, I didn't know anybody. So I started rebelling and accumulating minor naval charges for disobeying orders, not turning up to duty when I was supposed to be there, backchatting, silly little things. Then it was put to me that if I didn't pull my socks up within thirty days I would be discharged. The Captain had my parents on the phone [and] my dad said, 'If you get kicked out, don't come back here, I'll flog you senseless'. I didn't want to be an officer; I just wanted to be a mechanic.

I basically pulled my head in and got through it. Within a month I shone; my grades lifted and my attitude changed. On my passing-out parade I wanted my whole family to come over and see it, because it was a big thing. Mum and my younger brother and my grandmother came over, but I do remember I was absolutely devastated and heartbroken because my father wasn't there, he couldn't make it. I was doing all this for him and he wasn't even there to enjoy the spoils. That really crushed me.

To an outsider, Stuart's childhood is a typical example of suburbia in Sydney's south-west; his father was a brick-layer and his mother a homemaker. When I first asked Stuart about his family, he painted a rosy picture.

STUART: I think my childhood life was quite good. I had very caring parents. I'm the youngest in the family; I've got two older sisters, [who] are fourteen and sixteen years above me.

When I pressed further about his parents, however, a different picture emerged. I learnt, for example, that Stuart's father had spent three years as a prisoner of war in Singapore during Word War II and had had difficulty adjusting to civilian life on his return.

STUART: They were cold. My parents were very cold. They used to argue. Mum used to run off into the bedroom in tears. Dad was, I think, showing the pain from war. The pain was coming out in slow, small doses ... little things would stress him out ... he used to go to the hotel and have a couple of drinks— not overdo it, just a couple of drinks—and I think that was a trigger for that little bit of anger to come out. Sometimes it got a bit more than just a bit.

AUTHOR: Did your dad talk to you about his war experiences?

STUART: Not in the early part of my teenage years, but recently he's started to let go of the pain and I'm starting to understand him more. It helps me realise how much he's gone through. And I think in recent times, because of the trauma that I've been going through, he's been able to release that anger and talk about it without just holding back. He can understand where I'm going and I can understand where he's been. I think he would have done it [his time as a POW] a lot harder but he knows what I'm thinking and how I'm feeling and what it's going to do to me.

For Gordon, violence was something he experienced daily; it was part and parcel of his upbringing and considered normal.

GORDON: I had a very disciplinary father. My two older sisters were great. My older brother was just a turd. Because I was the youngest and I was the baby boy with the angelic curly hair, I got all the attention, and that put his nose out of joint. So he wasn't how a big brother should have been, like I see these big brothers on TV; and even the ones that muck around with their little brothers—it was nothing like what I had to go through. I had violence in my life every day just about.

AUTHOR: What do you mean? He beat you up every day?

GORDON: Yeah, until I got old enough to retaliate, you know, and then the shoe was on the other foot.

Gordon, like Stuart, did not mention his father's violence until prompted.

GORDON: He was a strict disciplinarian. There was no leeway with him where I was concerned. I got belted; I'd get about two or three beltings a week with the strap. It was bad. You know the strap that barbers used? That was the razor strap. It had that silver hook on the end that they'd hook onto the loop, right? Sometimes I'd cop the end of that; it'd break skin.

AUTHOR: Was it open cuts and bleeding?

GORDON: Sometimes.

AUTHOR: Did you feel loved?

GORDON: From my mother, yeah.

AUTHOR: And from your father?

GORDON: Nah, I'd say nah. It was like living in a mine-field. I was always scared of him. I suppose maybe I was an arsehole of a kid, you know, I was always getting into trouble. But that was just kids' stuff.

I'll tell you a story, right? This kid, I think I was about eight or nine and he was about seven, and he had this little twenty-four inch frame pushbike, right? And it had flat tyres and he didn't know how to do it, so I showed him. Fixed the punctures, put it back together, pumped it up for him and I said, 'Can I borrow it to go down to the shops? I'll get us cigarettes'. I've just gone and had a bit of a roll around the park, come back, got the drinks and as I was coming home my next door neighbour says, 'Your dad's looking for you. That young kid up the road has come down and said you've nicked his bike'.

That was bullshit, right? And I knew there wasn't going to be no leeway with my father so I went behind the shops, I got cardboard and I tore it up into strips and I put it down the back of me pants. I got home and there's his strap there. Anyway, to cut a long story short, I got grabbed by the scruff and whack, whack, whack, and luckily I didn't move because if he had've got my legs, well, they were unguarded 'cause I had shorts on. So it was just shit like that, mate.

AUTHOR: Did you ever think of running away?

GORDON: Oh yeah, which day? But that would have only hurt my mum. I have to say, my mum and dad are the two most honest people I've ever come across. I'm not saying that because they're my parents; they're the two most honest people, truthful.

AUTHOR: Do you talk to your dad about the past?

GORDON: Dad's dead. I could never talk to my father. I was scared of him. How could I talk to someone I was scared of? He could turn right on me with a word. That's a sad relationship.

AUTHOR: Did you ever discuss it in his later years?

GORDON: Well, my dad started seeing what I was going through with the police, right? This is where he started seeing that they were liars. It was after I did my first prison sentence. I was genuinely making an effort not to do anything, but because someone that the police were after was an old school friend of mine they came after me. They charged me with robbery in company and all the evidence they had was a bong and a syringe and Dad said, 'How did they charge you with that?' That afternoon we were putting the canvas and that on the sunroof on the back patio, and he said, 'But you were with me ... that ain't right'. And I said, 'It's the way it's always been, Dad. I'd [I've] been telling you this shit for years and you've been giving me beltings'.

Darren grew up in a suburb in Sydney's west, an area that is over-represented in our jail population.

DARREN: Not a very nice place to live, where I'm from in western Sydney. It's a dirty place; it's filthy; everything is either burnt or trashed. People lived there in fear, not being able to walk outside after six o'clock at night. If they did they could have problems.

AUTHOR: What was your childhood like?

DARREN: It was difficult but also fun. Basically, my mother was strict. I wasn't allowed out past our circle where we lived. It was a little cul-de-sac. That was like a safe haven. We could rely on each other and what not. But as I kept getting older, around eleven, I wanted to run around and do what I wanted to do, breaking into houses and taking things off the line— that's what everyone did; there was nothing there, absolutely nothing for people. We haven't even got a tennis court, we haven't got a youth centre. So the only thing that we could do was to make our own fun. It's the environment, basically—if you want to stay here your kids are going to grow up thieves and bad people. There's not too many people there that haven't thieved.

AUTHOR: What was your family like?

DARREN: My family life was better than most. Always had meals on the table, always had a bed, clean house all the time, fresh clothes. There was a lot of love, a lot of caring within our place.

AUTHOR: What were your parents like?

DARREN: My dad, he ran off with another woman and that. He used to come home from work drunk and bash Mum for many, many years. One day Mum got her own back; when he was drunk, bashed him and kicked him and threw him out in the street and said, 'That's enough'. I was four or five then.

AUTHOR: Was he ever violent towards you?

DARREN: Once. I rang my stepmother, who works in a bank. And she told Dad and Dad come home and backhanded me and sat on me, knocked me over, sat on my chest, started slapping me and I pissed myself, shouting, 'Get off me, Dad, get off me'. He said, 'I told you not to use the phone'. I don't think his wife liked me. [I] used to go to his place for school holidays; I used to choose him over my mum until I'd seen the real him.

AUTHOR: What do you mean?

A Bad Start

DARREN: I think I was eleven, and one night he went down the pub, got drunk, come back and started crying on my shoulder and what not. 'I want your mother back.' I said, 'No, you're no good for her'. I said, 'Look at yourself, you're a bum'. I said, 'Mum didn't want anything to do with you and I don't want anything to do with you'. He got very savage and called her a slut [and] this and that.

Darren was the only inmate I interviewed who was still openly angry with his father—not, however, for the way his father treated him, but on his mother's behalf.

DARREN: After he called Mum that name I would have liked to—and still would like to—pull his heart out. One day when I'm big enough I probably will. Until that day I don't want to see the man or acknowledge him. I've only seen the man three times in the last fifteen years. Last time I saw him was probably just over eight years ago, just before I was brought down here. I'm not too concerned about him, I honestly don't care if the man dies tomorrow. I hate him.

AUTHOR: Has he tried to contact you?

DARREN: He's tried to contact me; he had a private investigator run around trying to find me and what not. He never found me, which is quite bizarre because I'm stuck in jail.

AUTHOR: What about your mum?

DARREN: My mother, she did the best that she could and I love her and respect her for that. She used to *work; Dad also used to help out, come over and give us a bit of food or $40 or whatever it was back then. Food was always there, you never went to the fridge or the cupboard and there wasn't anything in it. Most families that I know are basically not too concerned about that with their kids, which is horrible to see, because I would invite their kids up to my house and Mum would wash them up a bit, give them a feed. I might not have got pocket money or lollies but I still had the right food with the right books, the hair done and the shoes polished. These kids didn't.*

AUTHOR: Did she used to drink?

DARREN: When I was younger she loved to drink, don't worry about that. I've looked after Mum when she's been drunk and vomited in her bed. I don't know how old I was, could have been nine, could have been what-ever, but I picked her up and put her in the bath, undressed her, dressed her and changed the sheets. I don't mind doing that, that's my mum, you know what I mean? She pulled me up the other week on a visit, she goes, 'That's a burden for you'. I said, 'Mum, many sons do it, of course I'm going to look after you'.

We had a lot of parties at home with a lot of rough men and what not. But they weren't violent, they were just hectic and loud and tore the place up. It was good because the next morning I'd go and check behind the lounge for money, so I enjoyed it. They'd go for two, three days sometimes. That was Mum.

The level of incarceration of Indigenous Australians is staggering. Prison is arguably the only public institution in which Aboriginal Australians form the largest group and, as shall be seen later, dominate. While Aboriginal Australians make up only 2 per cent of the New South Wales population,[21] they make up more than 15 per cent of the state's prison population.[22]

Prior to my conversations with prison inmates, I had seldom spoken with Indigenous Australians and my knowledge of their circumstances was purely academic. David and Michael, however, confirmed much of what I had read and heard. To them the stolen generations is not an episode that occurred long ago and the debate surrounding it is not something they witness from the sidelines. Rather, it is an accurate description of their mothers' lives. David and Michael grew up on the fringes of Australian society— even, in some ways, outside it.

DAVID: I'm from up north originally, born on the mission up there. My dad is Irish. It's a bit of a long story between my mum and dad. My mum was from the stolen generation; she was from Western Australia and she was taken up towards Queensland, where my dad ran into her. They were teenagers and they ... ran away together and got married there. They had six boys and two girls, and I'm the second youngest out of the boys and I've got two sisters younger than me.

Before they had kids my dad took my mum to where she was from, to her real people in Western Australia. She was taken away when she was four and a half, and that was the first time she'd seen her sisters, her brothers, her mother and that. They didn't recognise her at first. I think it was my grandmother's aunt that recognised her from a tribal mark from when she was a little girl, a scar across her ankle where she cut her foot open or something. It was very emotional for her. A couple of my mum's sisters were taken away all over Australia and just in the last couple of years she ran into them.

My mum and dad stayed up there for a couple of years and had a couple of my older brothers, and then they come down back to New South Wales. I grew up in Waterloo and there were a lot of places where we weren't allowed to go with my father, there were a lot of places in the city where I wasn't allowed in. Like in the sixties and early seventies we weren't allowed in the picture theatres. It was whites only and we had our own picture theatre out La Perouse way that was just for Kooris. So it was very racist and pretty hard for us. That's why I always had that hate of whitefellas. People making fun of my colour and I thought there was really something wrong with me. I used to go home to my mum and dad and cry, 'What's wrong with me?' and I used to get in the bath and try to scrub my colour off. They told me not to get mad: 'If you get mad you're only falling into whiteman's ways'.

Then a lot of my uncles from Ireland come to Australia and they toughened us up in the boxing ring and got us right into sports. Since we knew how to feed ourselves and do our own shoelaces my dad would say, 'You've got to be tough, you've got to be tough'. That's just the way it was. My dad was a professional boxer, so was my grandfather, and they brought that onto us. Then we realised what damage we can do with our hands. We just turned to violence straightaway. If someone had a go at us we'd have a go straightaway. That's how it was when I was young, nine, ten or eleven.

AUTHOR: What kind of man was your father?

DAVID: Dad's very hard, strict in rule, very strict, a man of few words, never talked about his feelings. 'Don't cry in front of women because that's a poof; you want to cry, go and put a dress on' and 'You don't tell on no-one' and stuff like that. When we were young, me and my brothers, if something happened around the house my dad used to say, 'Who done that?', and we used to say, 'It was him', so he'd belt him and belt all of us for telling on him. He just taught us that way, really toughened us up.

The fear is still there with my father. He comes out and visits every four or five weeks. I don't think my father's ever told me that he loves me but I can just tell by the way he goes on, little things he does; he stands by me.

AUTHOR: And your mum?

DAVID: Me mum is excellent, she still treats me like a baby. When she comes out to visit me she looks behind my ears, checks my teeth, wipes stuff off my face with her spit on the hanky and stuff like that. I love her for that. Always tell my mum I love her. It's easy to do that to my mum, she's just a woman's woman.

AUTHOR: How did they get along?

DAVID: They never argued, not in front of us, I've never seen them argue. My dad used to be a bit of a drinker when we were young and I think my mum gave him the ultimatum—'the drink or us'—and my dad went to us. That's how I know my father loves me, he just doesn't say it. They're still together.

Life Behind Bars

During one of our conversations, David told me something I found difficult to comprehend. We were talking about schooling when he mentioned that he only learnt to read and write when he first came to prison. I later discovered that it is not uncommon for inmates to be unable to read and write; the illiteracy rate in NSW prisons is 20 per cent compared to a state average of 3 per cent.[23]

David's parents and teachers were unaware of his inability to read or write throughout his primary and secondary school years. School attendance was not considered a priority in his life. He explained how he was led to believe that our education system is more a tool of white propaganda than a necessity for a bright future.

> DAVID: Didn't worry about school, we used to think they're trying to brainwash us in whiteman's ways. We used to say 'Our grandmother is sick' or 'Me uncle is sick up north so we're going away for a couple of months', so we had a month off school and we'd go back for two or three periods and do it all again. I didn't learn how to read and write till I was nineteen. One day I was home and my dad asked me what was on TV; he passed me the TV guide and I just didn't know. My dad looked at me and said, 'Get up on the table' and he's grabbing my ear, he's pulled me up and he's grabbed all my brothers and all that, 'Can youse read? Well, you read this to me'. Probably if he didn't ask me I would have got away with it for a couple more years. My mum was disgusted, she was deadset disgusted. We used to go to school only once a week and that was on sports day, because we were good footballers. They got their sporting stuff up so they didn't worry about us.

A lack of emphasis on education was common in the homes of the inmates. Darren's schooling was also largely ignored, and the fact that he was an underachiever did not help matters.

DARREN: Didn't worry about school, mate. I was very bad at school. I was below grade, not the normal classes, the underachievers. But it wasn't just me, it was all my friends in that class. It was good—we all ran amuck, we got caned, we got kicked out of class, we did what we wanted to do. We give the teachers hell and what are they going to do? Kick us out of school?

AUTHOR: What did your mum do?

DARREN: Mum got annoyed but it didn't really bother me. Now I think I should have listened at school but it's a bit too late for that now. I can read and write, not good but enough to get me through. Big words are a bit hard.

Michael was the second Indigenous inmate I spoke with. He matter-of-factly described being born to a teenage mother and abusive father. As a child Michael was shuffled between relatives, depending on domestic circumstances.

MICHAEL: My mother was fifteen and a half, my dad was sixteen, when I was born. The welfare wanted to take me off my mother, said my mother was too young, being Aboriginal and with a white government, and my aunty came and grabbed me from the hospital and took me before they realised what was going on. I stayed with my aunty till I was about two. My mother came and seen me all the time. I didn't know all this then; I would have only been a baby.

My mum sort of lived there too but she had to go to work and I think that was in the city, and my mother and father got a house in the inner city. I was nearly three when I went and lived there, till I was about four and a half. My mum was working with the Aboriginal Development Commission and we got a housing loan from the Land Council, bought a house about a kilometre from my aunty and we lived there till I was about five, five and a half.

AUTHOR: How did your parents get along?

MICHAEL: My father used to abuse my mother physically, and I think she had enough; I remember one Saturday he came back from a fete and assaulted her and I was hiding behind the chair and my mum grabbed me and we ran down to my aunty's house. My father left, and from that day on it was just me and my mother and my aunty, my mother's younger sister. We lived there till I was about seven, then my mum had to go overseas to Canada and San Francisco for work for six months and I went back with my aunty, with my eldest aunty that originally took me from hospital, because my youngest aunty was too young to look after me.

My youngest aunty couldn't handle me. Like, I would have been eight or nine and I started not coming home on the weekends, started getting an alcohol problem; like, working all week and then staying in at the weekends and coming home maybe Sunday or something, to get clothes and that. I used to see my mum every now and then. I got in trouble at eleven for driving cars in a car yard, playing smash-up dudes, and I got charged and my father came in and my mother wasn't getting her life together and my father said he'd take me, so I went and lived with him.

AUTHOR: Had you seen him throughout this time?

MICHAEL: Maybe once a year, sometimes twice a year, just depends. Sometimes I wouldn't even see him at Christmas. But I went and lived with him, changed high schools.

AUTHOR: How did you get along with him?

MICHAEL: My father pushed me away from home when I got expelled from school. He worked all his life and I respect him for that. I didn't understand at the time but my grandfather, his father, died when he was young and he had to take over his younger brother and sister and his mother and look after them, so he worked on the council since he was fifteen. And when he didn't have me he used to drink a lot, but then when I came to live with him he stopped drinking through the week and only drink [drank] on the weekends. I'd get expelled from school, suspended from school, and would hear nothing about it. At the time he'd come and pick me up and he'd be stressed and angry, for sure, but he wouldn't do nothing about it, he'd just send me to my room and that was that. But then on a Friday after work he'd go have a drink with his mates and come home and belt me and by that time it was a different feeling.

AUTHOR: Were you scared living with him?

MICHAEL: I was scared of getting in trouble and him finding out. The third time it happened I just said, 'Fuck this shit' to myself and I just ran. I just stepped around him, flew out the door, grabbed my bike and I rode to my mum's and grandpa's and I stayed there. My mum was saying, 'You've got to go home, you've got to go home', and I said, 'I'm not doing nothing. Fuck, you go home and cop the floggings'. If anyone could understand I thought my mother could understand; she's been there, you know what I mean? And Mum said, 'Look, you got in trouble', and I said, 'Yeah, fair enough, slap me around the head with an open hand, but, you know, he nearly knocked me out'.

As I got older and more confident in my own ability I did ring him from police stations and he did come and pick me up from boys' homes. I was always intimidated but it grew less and less over time.

AUTHOR: You just went from home to home to home, essentially, you were passed around your family.

MICHAEL: I don't really think about it. That was just how it was since I was young. Maybe I was accustomed to it. Maybe because it happened from an early age I just thought it was a part of life for me. But I know that where I went I was always loved.

My aunty had a lot of children of her own, plus she had my mother's younger brothers and, originally, my younger aunty that was living with her. So I was the baby of them and I got mollycoddled but I used to cop it from the elder children; that taught me a lot.

Both Michael and David were instilled with fear of white society from birth. David was afraid of being kidnapped by white men in uniforms—it was a threat he took seriously, as it was precisely what had happened to his mother.

DAVID: We were very scared of the police. When we used to see them we used to think they were going to take us away so we used to run from them. They had one of the coppers on a horse in front of the school and so we couldn't go in the front, had to sneak in from the back. Used to hate it. It was scary, very scary. Especially what my mum used to tell us: 'Never trust a whitefella. The only whitefella you can trust is your father because your father is not like that'.

I still do that here today. I'll trust a blackfella before a whitefella, it's just the way I think. When I'm around blackfellas we laugh. We laugh at anything, make things up to make us laugh, we like to be happy all the time. But when I'm with other people I'm very quiet.

As a child, David lived in the bush for some time among his mother's clan and immersed in traditional Aboriginal life. Despite the immense poverty he experienced during this period of his life, he recalls it as a happy time.

DAVID: Me mum's mum I only met a couple of times, when we went to WA. She lived on the mission in a tin shack. This was when I was seven to ten. Grandma used to tell me a lot of sacred stories about our sacred ground, the land, stuff like that. She was very strong, she was the boss. In Aboriginal life your mother can be your grandmother, your aunty, all the women of the family; they all treat you like you're their own. And I remember all my family used to look up to her because she was the oldest, she was everybody's grandmother. I called her Mum.

I remember my aunty was telling me that when they were young the men would work in the railways and that's when the people would come in, the nuns and that. They used to come in and say, 'She's sick, we've got to take the little girl to hospital' and they used to take them that way, send them everywhere and never bring them back. It was mainly the Church—they thought they was doing the right thing because they didn't think we were living right, because we were living on the land. Makes me mad, makes me really angry. It's hard.

AUTHOR: What was it like living there?

DAVID: Growing up on the mission was unreal. All around you are people that love you. You're living next to your aunties and all your cousins. The family was real close. We used to live in a tin shed just a little bit bigger than this room, all sleeping all over each other and my aunties and that in it. It was a good life, I loved it, I don't regret it one bit. My uncles from up that way used to go out hunting and we used to eat a lot of vegetables and once every two weeks they used to kill the animals, kangaroos and all that and throw them on the fires and that was our meat for three weeks. Mainly just fishing, living off fishing.

AUTHOR: Why did you leave?

DAVID: I think my dad wanted to get out of the mission for us kids, get us an education, because we didn't do any school.

AUTHOR: How did you adjust to your new home?

DAVID: I spun out when I first come to Waterloo; that was very scary, it was hard. There wasn't many black people there; they used to look at us real funny, and my brother and sisters, we used to all eat together, mainly scared of them. They'd hardly ever seen an Aboriginal. We just knocked about together. We had to look after the girls, that was our number one rule that Dad said: we couldn't let the girls get out of our sight. If they go to the toilet you had to go with them and wait outside the door. My dad was very strict that way.

Michael spent his life in the city and was less exposed to Aboriginal rituals and traditions than David. Michael's sense of identity is nevertheless strong, driven partly by the prejudice and fear he experienced as an Indigenous Australian.

MICHAEL: I learnt that there's us and them and they don't like us. They don't want to kill us but they don't want to give us nothing. They give looks that say we don't deserve nothing, we're all scum, we're all drug addicts, alcoholics, we're no good to ourselves.

I knew what had happened, what had been done to my mother's side of the family. They wanted to take me away from my family when I was little, I knew that, it was instilled in me at a young age. I knew that Mum had to be careful, or that was what I was told, and I didn't like older people.

AUTHOR: And what does it mean to be Aboriginal?

MICHAEL: It means ... it's unique, special. I don't know, it's special to me. I see the strengths we have, the unity, the bond. I look at other nationalities and they don't have the strength and the bond.

AUTHOR: What is the common factor?

MICHAEL: I think it's the journey that all our ancestors have gone through together and that helps that strong bond, that strength and security to be together. To me it's just special; it's hard to put into words really. The culture is special to me, it's unique, mate, and you don't see other cultures doing those things that we do. I want to know but I don't know about Arnhem Land and the full bloods really, what their beliefs are.

AUTHOR: How do you think Australians in general feel about Aboriginals?

MICHAEL: To be honest, I think they think we get a free ride. They think we get everything given to us, that we self-destruct. But at least some of them would have that soft spot to actually have the empathy for what we went through, what our ancestry went through.
I know a lot because I'd heard it coming from them. Especially me being quite fair, they're unaware that I'm Aboriginal, some of them, you know what I mean?

David's childhood could best be described as marginalised. White society was a place in which he felt neither welcome nor a sense of belonging. He learnt to hate white people, despising them for despising him.

DAVID: Around five years ago I was fairly racist, very racist. The only white people I didn't mind was the Irish people but otherwise I hated whites.

How then did he react to the news that one Sunday morning in 2000, hundreds of thousands of Australians from all walks of life took part in a nationwide march to affirm their desire for reconciliation with Aboriginal Australians? Didn't he feel that these people were on his side? David answered this question with uncharacteristic emotion, explaining how that moment was an epiphany for him and many Indigenous inmates.

DAVID: Being honest, it only just changed since I seen that march, the walk over the bridge. A lot of us Kooris watched it and we couldn't spot a blackfella; it was just unreal for us. Couldn't believe how many white people were supporting us. One of us, the older Koori, he's from up where my people is from and he said, 'See, it's not the whitefellas, it's the government'. And we all looked at each other because there were that many people there. A couple of the older Kooris started crying. It was a big day for us.

When speaking with the inmates it was impossible not to feel that, given different circumstances, they would have taken a different path. As children they were certainly boisterous, some even later diagnosed as hyperactive, but they nevertheless showed promise for a successful future.

SHANE: I was very good at school. They'd put work in front of me and ten minutes later I was finished. Then I'd have to sit there for an hour and a half till recess and then lunchtime, then the afternoon. So I'd have to sit there for an hour and I was always a hypo kid, so that's where I'd get into trouble.

My son's been diagnosed with ADHD. My mother used to say, 'Sit down, eat your tea' all the time. I was called a bad tempered little bugger. I've always got to be moving. But now, now I can kick back.

MICHAEL: I listened in class, I was a good student. In the playground I was a bit different 'cause I was like captain of the cricket team, captain of the soccer team. I used to have arguments and fights and that in the playground but when it came to class time in primary school I always put my head down, done good work and my report card would show that. But when I got to high school, maybe sixth class, I started wagging a bit; things just fell apart.

Had things been different for Gordon and David, they may have become renowned for their sporting abilities, perhaps even playing professionally.

AUTHOR: Were you a sportsman?

GORDON: Yes, oh yeah, rugby union. I got picked for district, the under-fifteens. But you needed $1200 to go on an excursion to New Zealand and my parents didn't have the money. I couldn't ask them. But I still played. I'd play my game, then I'd go play for the under eighteens, right? I'm a thirteen-year-old kid and I'm playing for the under eighteens.

At one stage David was contracted to play first grade rugby league for a Sydney-based team.

DAVID: I represented Australia in rugby league, played over New Zealand, went to England. I wanted to just be a rugby league player, and rugby league players, you know, they're as thick as bricks and it used to suit me fine. I never really worried about anything else.

I played for them [the Sydney club] one season but I broke my collarbone and I never played for them no more, I just played first division up in the bush. I was breaching my contract because I still owed them three or four months of football and when they found out I was playing up there they can sue the club so I had to stop playing. It didn't worry me because I was in with the drugs and that too. Drugs were more important. When I watch football today and I see a lot of the first graders and I used to play with them—it could have been [me], but I didn't really worry about it that much.

As the next chapter shows, these signs of a potentially bright and law abiding future were merely islands of optimism. Overwhelmed by drugs, alcohol, violence and crime, the pull towards hedonism and self-destruction was too strong and was to set the course for the years to come.

Chapter 3:
Getting Worse

With intermittent schooling and little supervision, all the inmates had become familiar with the law by the time they reached their teens. Left to their own devices, they were lured into trouble. And while teenhood could be defined by the pushing of boundaries, most teens are able to confine their behaviour within acceptable social boundaries and avoid jeopardising their futures. The inmates I spoke with had no such constraints or considerations; their teenage years were marked by an indifference to what most of us regard as basic social values and to their own futures.

> JASON: I was pretty uncontrollable as a kid, getting into trouble. Actually, I found out later that I had ADD. I don't use that as an excuse but it does explain things. I just couldn't stay focussed on anything for very long, I got bored easy so I'd get up to mischief. Probably at thirteen, fourteen, I was stealing a bit from shops and at fifteen I did a few other things like break-and-enter and a couple of drug charges for pot. I was really impulsive, I didn't think of consequences, I'd just do something.

Jason's early years in a small country town culminated when he was asked to leave home at fifteen, leaving him to his own devices.

> JASON: My parents didn't want me to corrupt my little brother and sister, because the police were always

coming around and stuff like that. I ended up going into a refuge. For the next five years I just moved around from place to place and I think I was caught up in a cycle where if I moved it was a fresh start but I didn't realise my problems moved with me. It was only when I ended up in jail that I had to start dealing with my problems and facing them.

With little comfort to be derived from their erratic and violent homes and much adventure to be experienced elsewhere, all of the inmates I spoke with relied on neighbourhood friends to provide a sense of belonging. Among the boys, kudos and popularity were assured through feats of anti-authoritarianism.

STUART: I always thought [of] myself [as] a follower, not a leader. I was a follower, wanted to be part of what they were doing and not thinking about consequences. We experienced drugs, experienced alcohol.

When you're that young you don't realise, 'Well, this is wrong'. You got to be part of the era, you know, what the boys are doing. You've got to copycat or else they'll just, you know, they'll push you aside, you'll not be part of the group anymore. And you want to prove to yourself that you're just as capable of doing what they do, make a name for yourself. And those influences that I got from my school sent me on the wrong road, to disaster. It's a road and a choice that I did not realise I was taking until I grew with wisdom and got the knowledge I have today.

AUTHOR: What kind of crowd were you in?

STUART: It was the in crowd. See, there were many groups but it was the one where you get a name for yourself. You didn't want to miss the action. It made you feel like you were part of the boys. And you were just creating havoc for yourself, smoking pot, not staying home, late nights out at the boys' houses, skipping school. But that didn't really start until it got to a stage where ... there was something better than school, like going to the beach.

Stuart experienced his first run-in with the law at fifteen, when he broke into a school and stole some stationery and calculators to gain status among his friends.

STUART: I don't know why I done it. I still don't even know why. It was just a thought that I could do it. I took a couple of calculators, not much, just, like, quick things.

AUTHOR: Is that what the other guys did?

STUART: Yeah, well that was it. They'd talk about their crimes and other stuff like that. I thought, well this is an opportunity, no-one's around. The problem was that while I was in the building the teacher's come to do a bit of Saturday work. And that was the first time I had any sort of run-in with police and trouble and crime, because I was caught red-handed. And it should have just told me then, it should have given me some sort of description that I was getting vulnerable to those influences.

AUTHOR: What happened next?

STUART: I got taken to the police station. I got charged with break and enter and it was the first time someone's ever had to call my parents and say, 'We've got your son down here at the police station'.

AUTHOR: Did they know that you had an alternate life?

STUART: No, they didn't. They used to warn me and say, 'Look, you shouldn't go to that. He's bad. He's bad'. But you ignored it and you copped the crap later. When you come home and they're saying, 'You shouldn't have been out there. We're going to do this to you'. And you keep doing it ... because you are used to getting away with it and getting away with it. It became a natural part of life, so you just ignored it.

I knew I was going to face the music when I got home; but facing the music got less and less of a trauma. And you're getting off and there's no consequence for it. My parents' sort of values were starting to limit me and I thought that I was getting big enough to look after myself. They used to listen to excuses and used to just make a comment about the excuses and that was it.

AUTHOR: Do you think you could have been punished into behaving better?

STUART: I think if they were harsh on me I would have rebelled against it, because I wasn't looking at the future, wasn't looking at where am I heading. I was just rebelling against them, just because I thought there was something better. I was putting all the most important things in my life up on the shelf and not going forward. All I was doing was staying in the same sort of environment.

AUTHOR: No dreams, no aspirations?

STUART: No dreams, no career, nothing, no goals. Just to prove yourself, just to prove to your mates that, you know, you're someone good to hang around with.

AUTHOR: So you get taken to the police station ...

STUART: The police threw the White Pages *at me and I heard that* White Pages *were being used as a sort of a cushion against blows so I got a bit, very scared. I asked, 'What do you want me to do with the phone book?' He goes, 'I want you to look up your parents' phone number'.*

My father came to the police station and saw me sitting there and [the police] explained what I had done. I think that was enough to sort of say to himself, 'Right, now I've got to put my foot down or this is going to continue'. And I could see in my parents that it was very disturbing to see their son starting to go off the rails. And they tried as hard as they could to earbash me about what happened and it stuck. It stuck because I was on a good behaviour bond for eighteen months.

AUTHOR: Were you scared?

STUART: Oh yeah, of course you were scared. You don't realise the consequences until you're faced with the consequences and that frightened me. I still was off the rails but it was enough for me to say, 'I've got to be more careful in what I'm doing'. It was just go back to school and pretend it's not happened and we'll get back into a rhythm and start again.

I had to be trouble-free because I was straight to the boy's home if I'd been caught again. But I was still in the same groups, same environment and people. I decided I was going to lay off a bit. I was quite good at school. But then when the influences started to take their toll again, my grades started dropping. I used to do homework for the first two years of high school, I was an A-grade.

AUTHOR: I'm guessing that to other guys you hung around with, grades didn't really matter?

STUART: No. Their grades were at the bottom; dunces of the school.

AUTHOR: You didn't fit that mould perfectly?

STUART: No, but you get pulled in by the magnet of these people at school. You get pulled in that circle because you want to get known. And it's very frightful not to be known. It's just like you're a wimp or something like that, not being involved. And that's how I got pulled down. And by the time I was up to my school certificate I'd gone from top grades down to sort of less than average grades. But I was happy with that.

I decided [that] once I got my school certificate I'd go onto year eleven. I got my school certificate and I thought that was a big achievement in itself. I thought that I wanted more, I thought I was capable of doing my Higher School Certificate.

I got my driver's licence. I think it was a big step in my life, a turning point. That gave me freedom. My father gave me a car and I took it to school. I thought, 'Here I've got something, a vehicle that I can use for freedom; why am I here at school when I don't have to be at school? I'm grown up and can make decisions now'. I used to turn up at school and I used to think, 'Do I really want to learn today or do I really want to go to the beach?'

Most of my mates had left school. The ... smart ones and the ones that wanted to sort of achieve something stayed on. So I was spending three days out of five at school; two days were becoming the drive around town, get up to mischief or go and see things, do your own thing, live your own life. And by the end of year eleven the big question came from the headmaster and he says, 'Do you really want to be here?' And it was a shock because I'd never had to face the headmaster. And he said, 'Listen. Your attendance is quite down. Now the only proposition I've got for you is either you repeat year eleven or you leave'.

So I left school and spent a couple of months playing around. And my parents started earbashing me again about 'Now you're not at school, what are you going to do?' So I decided to take up a pre-apprenticeship as a motor mechanic.

AUTHOR: Were you into cars?

STUART: I was good with my hands and I felt I'd do something to do with motor mechanics. I got my own car, I can use my hands and I've watched Dad do it.
And away I went—I got in. And I did a pre-apprenticeship for a complete twelve months, going to tech and learning the trade, and I started getting very, very keen on it and at the end of that first year of that

apprenticeship I went out and I got a job with an employer who gave me a start.

AUTHOR: This new experience, did you feel restricted or did you feel proud?

STUART: I felt proud because I was doing something my old man was doing. I was getting somewhere. But I also didn't realise that it's a full commitment and that. The first three months I didn't realise, why am I getting all these terrible jobs? Because as a first-year apprentice you only get the terrible jobs. After a while you think, 'Do I really want to do this cleaning up and getting lunches and this and that?' I think I was getting $97 a week—it's gone within two days; it wasn't really very much.

So I gave up three months later. Actually, I got retrenched, I didn't give up. And another bloke gave me a start so I continued on and finished my apprenticeship and eventually started getting very experienced and getting the good jobs and I started to feel good about the job.

But I'd also gone through a lot of jobs, and those changes in life—getting new jobs and having to go and face new employers and telling them you're the best man for the job—was hard. Being retrenched from some of the jobs was hard. Having to leave some of the jobs was hard. In that sort of environment you start to lose your self-confidence again. And all I wanted to do was settle somewhere but not working as a mechanic any more. So I took on a driver's job and ... I worked as a spare parts driver for eight years, and that's the longest job I've ever had. And then I walked out. I thought, 'This is not for me'.

I was thinking about superannuation, long service leave and everything but I walked out before that. So I went and got another driver's job. But I've got a bit of a brain in my head, I can use a computer, so they'd taken me out of the car and put me in an office, a very responsible job, and started training me, and then the confidence came back. Now I've become sort of a field manager, having big responsibilities. And I felt good about myself. And I worked there for about two years and then this is where this problem came. This is where the crime came.

AUTHOR: Were you a violent person at that stage?

STUART: I got angry at times. I was hurting. Having to go to work, having to produce at my best ability, having bad things go down at the office and having to take it home and trying to leave it at the door but taking it inside the house with me. And when something bad happened I used that as an excuse for an explosion. I was blaming other people, not looking at myself, and this is what caused conflict and domestics. And I always thought I was right, you know?

AUTHOR: Were you in any trouble with the police?

STUART: I had the police come to my house for domestic violence. I got a bit over the top and threw my girlfriend around the house a couple of times. She was a bit frightened about it. The police attended and I said, 'I'm under the influence of alcohol'.

I had a few other run-ins with the police. Mostly I did assaults but I was never found. They were just sort of small violences but there were no repercussions from them.

The inmates all told similar stories of adolescences filled with alcohol, drugs and, eventually, crime. To them, violence was a norm they endured at home. The hurt, fear and anger they experienced found a panacea by way of substances that numbed their emotions, and they eventually became addicts. Their crimes started as an adventure to boast of later before their peers, but gradually crime turned into a lifestyle; an easy means of earning a living and feeding expensive habits. They seemed disinterested in anything beyond their immediate gratification and were oblivious to the consequences of their actions, not caring for the suffering of their victims or any punishment they may receive, if caught.

Intellectually the inmates saw their teenage years as wasted ones, which involved drug dependency and did nothing to advance them. However, in relating their adventures, I also noticed nostalgia for the good times that were had.

DARREN: My friends were mainly Kooris. They were my family outside Mum. I used to call their mothers and fathers 'Mum' and 'Dad' and they'd call me 'Son'.

My friends had been doing it for maybe eighteen months before me and they're like, 'We're doing a house, come and try it'. And I couldn't say no. Mum was really easy to get around. Like, I love her and respect her but when it comes to friends nothing is going to stop me. I just wanted to do whatever I wanted to. I was a very vindictive person when I was a kid, selfish for not doing what I was supposed to and wanting to rule my own roost. Now I think back, that was a little too much, I regret it.

Darren would leave home for days or weeks at a time, disappearing and reappearing intermittently. He described this stage of his life with emotion, but it was difficult to work out precisely what emotion that was. Relating an incident in which he almost murders his mother, he expresses guilt, but it seems fleeting.

DARREN: I kept leaving home to live on the streets with friends—this was just before my twelfth birthday— mucking around, smoking pot, drinking, hanging. Walking to the front gate at school and you might see one of your mates, 'Let's go, don't worry about school, mate'. Then I'd just take the school form to my Koori people and they signed [it] for me.

Eventually my mum had to kick me out for my own good because I was really aggressive, very Abo. I was just deadset wild. One night I went to a party, got drunk and the police picked me up, took me home, 'He was a menace, throwing bottles' and what not. As soon as they left I said, 'I'm going out, Mum'. Mum said, 'No you're not'. I said, 'I know better' and pulled a knife to her throat. And I said, 'You're either letting me out or I cut your throat ... I mean it'. I didn't know that my brother was home, and he just tapped me on the shoulder. I turned around [and] he knocked me flat out. Thank God, because I don't think Mum would be here.

They were mad days. I regret them but I don't. I just wish I could have done it different, maybe gathered around a support group. Back then my friends were just what I needed but I wouldn't call them friends now. I've woken up, I can see they were just using me because they could see I'd do anything. They were loving it because I was doing everything.

AUTHOR: Were you into drugs?

DARREN: I was an alcoholic by then, smoking pot, into speed. I used to thieve every day for me pot, for me alcohol. Speed wasn't a problem because I didn't pay for it. I've been on speed for, like, seventeen years now. At that age it's, like, most kids just experiment, but I was way past that stage, I was getting to thinking that this was going to be my life and I didn't want to change it.

AUTHOR: What kind of things were you doing?

DARREN: I was doing car thieving, break[ing] into houses, stealing motorbikes, walking down the shops and pinching pushbikes. And knowing I can get away with it is the ultimate.

AUTHOR: Did you ever have a job?

DARREN: I used to work. I worked as a trolley boy, stacking shelves. I went from there to a food processing plant ... for a couple of months. Basically, I've only had five or six jobs. Why work? Work's hard! I can get up at three o'clock in the afternoon, go out for ten minutes and make more money then you could earn all week. I don't see the point.

AUTHOR: Where were you living?

DARREN: I was sleeping everywhere, wherever I could lay my head. Every now and then I'd go home and have a feed, shower and go. Mum might see me five months later. I'll ring up, 'How you going? You all right?' Come home, have a feed, do the washing and I'd be gone in the morning. That's the way it was.

I ended up pinching the stereo and TV from my own home. I went straight from there to the drug dealer. Then I went home and the police were there doing fingerprints. I freaked, mind you, and never come back. When I did about two weeks later, my mum basically knew. I ended up telling her months later; that's when I decided to go into rehab. It didn't hurt me inside knowing that I robbed my family; it had to be done, it was so easy, people wouldn't suspect me because I lived there.

I ended up stabbing a Koori bloke in the stomach. He referred to my mother as a 'dog' so I stabbed him. I got three months for that. I was only sixteen or something. I went to juvenile home. I've been got for a few things before but got bails and bonds and orders, just all the crap that young juveniles go through. I suppose I was lucky, too, for not going to the home before, but I've surely made up for it in jail. I think if I would have done more juvenile time I would have been more unpleasant, done bigger and worse things.

AUTHOR: Why is that?

DARREN: Because the juvenile home I was in wasn't that bad. Used to get up and have a shower, beautiful food, watch TV till eight o'clock, and that wasn't bad. I never felt alone or abandoned. I can slot into any *situation, which is good. I don't know if many people can do it, mate, but I know I can.*

When the inmates were faced with violent homes, their friends became their protective units. And just like home, the street was a violent place to be. Most of Gordon's friends from his old neighbourhood are no longer alive.

GORDON: Out of the six of us that made up that unit, four of them are dead, one became a real Bible basher and I ended up here.

AUTHOR: How did the four die?

GORDON: Drug overdoses.

AUTHOR: Tell me about them.

GORDON: Left to my own devices, and my school friends that grew up in the area, that were my age, we sort of formed a gang. It was our gang, we stayed together through thick and thin.
We were like terrorists. A lot of my friends were in the same position, with older brothers that used to bash them. Well, what we used to do was, we'd get together and then we'd single out the offending brother. Then we can bushwhack them—give them a bad beating. This was the way we were.
So I had violence every day of my life and the violence I had at home, I used to take out on the street.

AUTHOR: Were you the ringleader?

GORDON: We were all individuals, we all had our ideas. But yeah, that's how I got the nickname 'The Cook'. You know they call me Cookie—I was always cooking up something to get into trouble.

AUTHOR: What kind of adventures did you have?

GORDON: We had a creek that used to run nearby, it went through a lot of industrial areas and the backs of these factories used to back onto this creek, and that was our creek, that was our domain.

And we were very good at pilfering. There was this drink company that backed onto the creek and they used to have this drainpipe for their water run-off. Well, we crawled up that and we'd come out in the factory. Then we'd start loading boxes of Coke, and we had like a trolley system going down to the creek. And then we'd sell it to the local shops—they were making money, we were making money and the local drink company, they never lost none.

There was also a spare parts place for bikes. We'd take a part here, a part there, and we'd build up a bike and then another one.

AUTHOR: What kind of things would flare up violence?

GORDON: If I was angry and had seen someone from the rival gang, that was fair game. But we only seemed to be battling bigger and older people. I went and fought my brother and his mates, and my mate and my friends and their brothers and their mates. You know, there was an ongoing war. It was war, mate. For toys I had a collection of slug guns; they were my toys. Knives too; I used to collect knives.

AUTHOR: Did these fights get dangerous?

GORDON: What do you perceive as dangerous? What you perceive as dangerous is different to what I perceive as dangerous.

AUTHOR: When it ends in hospitalisation.

GORDON: I think my parents got used to me being taken to hospital to get stitched up. My brother, we'd see him and his mates across the other side of the creek and they'd start, 'Get here, you little bastard'. And we'd shout, 'Fuck youse!' and we'd start rock fights.
   I was always getting into fights after school, and during school I'd get six-to-eighteen cuts a day. If I went a day without being caned, that was a good day.

As Gordon tells it, he became well known to the local police from as early as five years of age. He, like the other inmates, came to despise people in uniforms and the authority that they represented.

GORDON: There was one sadistic policeman. This cunt was bad news. He was just fucking off the planet, and he was a sergeant, right, and my first experience with him was when I was six, seven years old. He thought our gang was the troublemaking gang in the area and he wanted to keep his streets fucking clean. So he'd catch us one at a time, get the gun, the thirty-eight, at the back of the head, marched into the fucking little police station and then lock us into a broom closet. That was his thing.

I've been in police stations for fucking hours and hours getting beat up, and in the end the coppers give up in exasperation. I think the trick of it was, if you don't react to their punches and kicks and slaps, don't say a word, don't moan, groan, nothing, then they'll get frustrated; they'll try and beat you up even more but it will end quicker.

AUTHOR: When did the real trouble with the courts begin?

GORDON: The first time they really caught me, that was when I was fifteen. But until then it was nothing serious. Only because I hadn't got caught, I was really smart. But I was known to the police. I'd always go to other areas, I'd just jig school for the day. Me and my mates would go and I used to get into other people's houses just to see how they lived, to see if their life was the same as mine. I never took anything. I'd go to the fridge, I'd have a meal and I'd see what there was to eat. I don't know, I was a weird kid; I'm telling you, I was a weird kid.

AUTHOR: What happened when you were fifteen?

GORDON: Ah, the fuckers found fingerprints in a house. That's where I started to come undone. But I was doing other shit that I was making plenty of money from.

AUTHOR: Didn't your parents ever ask where you got money?

GORDON: Nah, I had cover stories, like the paper run; we used this good old one for fucking years.

Getting Worse

Fear and loathing of white authority figures was instilled in the Aboriginal Australian inmates like David and Michael at home at an early age. They did not feel bound by the law, which they felt was there to oppress rather than to protect them. While enjoying the reckless, materially rewarding lifestyle, they knew that the law they flouted so blatantly would catch up with them. They simply didn't care.

MICHAEL: I started smoking, hanging around the wrong people in high school. I got expelled in year seven and went back to my original high school. I got expelled from there about two months later and they brought me out to another high school. I didn't used to go; I'd have roll call in the morning and then take off. By this time I was hanging in the city with a lot of my cousins and that, a lot of friends, and none of them went to school.

AUTHOR: What did you guys get up to?

MICHAEL: We used to graffiti trains, search shops and hop tills and get money out of tills and back-room purses.

AUTHOR: Were you just having fun?

MICHAEL: Yeah, I was having fun. When you went out with your mates, you went to have fun and always a good life, always had money in my pocket.

AUTHOR: What drew you to the streets?

MICHAEL: I really can't pinpoint it. I know money was a big factor. I never ever had a lot of money and here

I was with a lot of money and living in motels. The women, too; like, I was just starting to get into women at that age and here they are. The city lifestyle, too; like, the pinball parlours, all-nighters sort of thing. Drugs wasn't really a factor till I was older.

AUTHOR: Is it easy to get money?

MICHAEL: The easiest way to get money is just grabbing it. From tills, from bank counters, from anywhere—just grab it and run. The easiest way to get a lot of money is to just rob a bank, quickest too—that's the easiest and the quickest.

Once you do the first one, the fear factor's broken down. You know what's supposed to be done and how to do it, you know where the coppers are coming from, you know what route to take.

AUTHOR: Who were your friends?

MICHAEL: As a thirteen-year-old, I used to hang around in town with a lot of mixed people. There was only me and a handful of us from around my area that were there. We used to do graffiti, we used to spray-paint a whole train; we had to steal the paint to do that. And that was, like, a thrill for us—like I was saying, as though I was stealing a car ... adrenaline rush. Had to get chased by train guards out of yards or wherever. Then I would go back to my cousins and my friends; like, the boys that I knew and grew up with. With the city boys we made a lot of money; with the inner-city boys we just sat around a lot. It was different, but I got on with both of them and I never had a problem with a mix.

But, with me, a lot of people didn't know that I was Aboriginal. I didn't care that my friends were white because my dad was white too.

Consider, too, what Michael had to contend with and make sense of in his home life.

AUTHOR: What was your relationship like with your mum throughout your teenage years?

MICHAEL: Distant probably. My mum was on heroin when I was eleven. I was doing my own thing but I used to see her around. She was stealing to support her habit. I'd seen her selling the stuff that she'd stolen and if I had a lot of money I said, 'Here, Mum'. But then, some days I'd have no money and she'd support me, too. Plus my little brother was around then too; he's a month older than my eldest daughter.

Sometimes I'd see Mum in the city thieving. I saw her trying to steal a watch, and that sort of thing. I didn't want her to go to jail and I knew my little brother would bear the brunt of it if she did go to jail. He was still a baby then. And that happened anyway and my grandfather looked after him, and my uncle.

The dysfunctional neighbourhood David described is situated only minutes from Sydney's central business district. So foreign is David's life to most Sydneysiders' lives, however, that even though many people travel past the area on their way to work, it may as well be a world away.

DAVID: We moved out of Waterloo because of the drugs. One of my older brothers found something in the school—I think it was just a bag that had some powder in it—and Dad was really against drugs. My brother didn't know nothing about it, he thought it was lollies, but when he tasted it, it made him sick. Once Dad found out it was a heroin, a week later we moved from there. It was getting done in the schools then; everyone was getting into the heroin around sixth class around Redfern/Waterloo.

Moving didn't stop us, because we all ditched school and went back in there, back to Waterloo, because that's where all the blackfellas were. We used to just walk around terrorising people every day. Used to be, like, ten of us, walking in a shop, taking the till, taking whatever we want and run out, do that all around the city. And that was our lives. Once we got into teenage years the violence used to get heavier, [we] used to knock around in a gang. You had your city gangs, like the skinheads, the punks and all—they were the ones we used to look for every night. We used to steal cars [and] drive into the city looking for them, and we used to just bash them with baseball bats.

I was surprised by David's candid descriptions of the senseless violence he perpetrated. By his teenage years, he had become a violent person and his actions were bereft of compassion or humanity. He and his friends were, in effect, lethal weapons, injuring and even killing those in their path.

DAVID: It was always bad when I was a teenager ... we used to go out looking for people just to bash. We got into poofter bashing, and we used to hurt a lot of them badly. Once one of them got really bashed bad and he died. That stopped it a bit. A lot of my mates are still doing jail for it today; some of them got thirteen years. That's when a lot of gay people were getting bashed to death. Well, I was in that, I was the one doing it. I don't know … it's the wrong thing and that. About three or four of them died from bashings, and all of us were under surveillance. I was on remand for around two-and-a-half years. After that, when I got out, it just made me hate everybody. Then the crimes I got into were aggravated robberies and armed robberies and stuff like that.

I was curious to learn what the inmates felt when committing their crimes. They knew they might go to jail, so the risk was high, but so too must have been the emotional rewards.

AUTHOR: Was it an adrenaline rush?

MICHAEL: Big adrenaline rush. I was withdrawing from heroin once and I was sick and I didn't want to get out of the car to do it, and when we pulled out of the car to do it I never felt sick the whole time I was in there, [but] not even a minute after I got back in the car I couldn't sit up properly in the back seat. And here I am running around normal—pure adrenaline rush—and then as soon as I got out of there and got back in the car I felt really withdrawn again.

Gordon, who had experienced violence regularly at home, also perpetrated it and I wondered why? What sensation did it give him?

GORDON: It's only lately that I've been really thinking about this, and it's because I was hurt so much that I liked to hurt other people. And strangers were fucking perfect, you know? But if you and I got to know each other then, nah, my loyalty knows no bounds.

AUTHOR: Have you hurt people during armed robberies?

GORDON: Nah, I don't have to. It's like I ooze menace when I'm doing it. Because I was exposed to this at an early age—having a gun pointed at me—I didn't consider that as violence. It's only when it went off that it was violence. So my attitude was: this is just a tool that's there. I didn't know that people seeing these guns could cause them so much terror.

AUTHOR: Did you get an adrenaline rush from committing robberies?

GORDON: Well, it's not so much going in and doing the robbery—that's cool, but it's the empty space when I come out and I could get into a gun battle. And that was the rush for me: the not knowing. I know that at the end of this job I'm going to be a little bit more comfortable with myself. I'd sit back, I'd go and have a nice hot shower, whatever. It's like I'd worked something out, the demons had been exposed: he's happy with what he's done and now he's sleeping. It's the only way I can explain it.

AUTHOR: It seems that if I met you on the right day at the right time, you'd be a fun bloke to hang around with, but if I met you at the wrong time I could be dead.

Getting Worse

GORDON: If on the wrong day you said the wrong thing … It all depends what the day was like. If we'd been sitting here smoking pot and you jumped up and said, 'Fuck you, fuck you', I'd just sit there laughing. But on another day, you couldn't; I'd be, like, 'Well, what's your go?' and I'd take it back to you. That was me being confrontational. I love that.

AUTHOR: But I get the feeling you were not completely without morals back then and that there were some things you regretted.

GORDON: I know, it's fucking weird, eh? There's one story, it's a true happening, right? And I've always remembered this and it's always made me feel like a bit of shit. Whenever I think of the bad things I've done in my life, this would be the main one, right? One of my gang was having a fight with someone from the other side of town. And they were down near the creek and they were getting into it and they were heading for the edge of the creek. Well, I've gone in to break them up and then I got punched from behind, right? Fuck, I just turned around and bang, like that, you know? It was a reaction, and it was this bloke's fucking sister, right? I gave her a purler. You know, it was just a reaction. Got her right in the mouth. I fucking knocked three of her teeth out, and all the bridgework had just been paid for. Conscience-wise, you know, it is a fucking regret that I'll have till the day I die, you know, even though it was accidental.

Gordon and Michael each spent a total of eighteen months in boys' homes during their teenage years. Life in these institutions was hard and unpleasant, but the time spent there did not result in a permanent change in their destructive behaviour—upon release, they did not have enough stability or positive influences to keep them from returning to their former lifestyles.

GORDON: I fucking hated them. But I did three of them so I mustn't have hated them too much, hey? But it wasn't a deterrent, you know; like, I adapted to that and I overcame [it]. When I'd leave boys' homes—get out—it's like, 'Fuck this'. I'd go interstate, I'd travel around, I used to get two or three jobs, then, when I'd come back to Sydney, it'd be the same environment, you know?

Michael was committed to a boys' home at fifteen for stealing a motor vehicle.

AUTHOR: What was it like?

MICHAEL: Terror of all sorts. I was intimidated and scared but I knew a lot of boys there, which helps. I just sat back and seen how things were run, who was who, and when I got all that down pat I'd come out of my shell.
  I had a really good run at boys' homes 'cause I've seen a lot of my friends go there for six months and then get out and they'd only be out for a month and then go back for twelve. I really only did one sentence. At the time I did try to regain my studies, and they had a college for Aborigines and I was studying the certificate, and the judge seen that and wanted to give me every benefit, I believe, to do that. That's why I kept getting bail, too, because some of the offences I had to get a sentence for—one was for possession

of a firearm. That was as a fifteen-year-old. That's a pretty serious offence.

I'd just come from the boys' homes; I got out a day before my eighteenth birthday. I recall the magistrate saying that he'll never see me again in a children's court. I was out for about a month and got pinched in a stolen car.

I knew in my head that I wasn't going to stop stealing. It was a lifestyle I'd become accustomed to. You could pick up $600 in five minutes. It was a lifestyle I knew I hadn't finished with yet. I knew I would come to jail and I knew a lot of my cousins and that were in here and friends.

Shane found himself in a seemingly impossible position, forced to choose between his pregnant girlfriend and his navy service. He absconded from the navy and was sentenced to Australia's least known and, as he described it, the most draconian of prisons—the military prison at Ingleburn in Sydney, run by the military rather than the Department of Corrective Services.

SHANE: I was sent to sea for two years to complete the practical side of the trade, and from the time I returned it's mostly been downhill since. Because I was away maybe nine months of the year at sea, my fiancée at the time gave me an ultimatum that 'It's either the navy or me—make your choice'. She then fell pregnant, and, being an adopted child and raised the way I was, I always said to myself that when I have a family of my own I want to raise the child, I want to be there for them and give them the love that I didn't receive.

I put in for a discharge and was knocked back. They'd spent so much money on training me they weren't prepared to let me go until I paid the time back. I wasn't happy with that so I took off, I shot through. If they can't find you after six months they just let you go. And I had been out for five months and two weeks when my parents rang the police and told them where I was going to be. They wanted me arrested; they decided that was best for me. To this day they swear they never did that; they won't admit that they give me up.

Anyway, I went to the military prison at Ingleburn. I was sentenced to ninety days, and it was hell. You've got to request permission for everything. You can't talk at all, ever. 'Pass me the salt' is a charge. If I get caught talking to you—bang!—seven-day charge. I remember sitting out the front of our cells in the afternoon to polish our boots; we'd sit there and talk without moving our lips. The officers were in the gatehouse sitting there with binoculars trying to see our lips move. If they could see us [talk] they would say over the PA: 'I can see you talking, you're charged'. No TV, no newspapers, no radios. If you go to the toilet they are standing right in front of you and there are no doors. Nothing in your cell except your uniform and boots. You'd have to lay your kit on your bed every morning, fold it a certain way, with a certain length. If there was one shirt or one button not done up, the whole cell would be tossed out and you'd have to re-do it all and if you didn't you'd be charged.

Physically they can't lay a hand on you but it's all mental fucking hell. They degrade you, they call you an animal and there is not a damn thing you can do about it. If I retaliate or say 'fuck', I'm charged. Every conceivable humiliating word you could think of they *ran by you daily. Their view is that any prisoner who comes through that establishment will be the perfect soldier when they leave: they are fully rehabilitated, complying with any order.*

I didn't want to be there any longer than I had to be, so I absorbed everything that was thrown at me. After that experience I made up my mind to get out of the navy. It was harder than the ten years I've done here, the psychological torture they inflict on you.

Shane was emotionally unstable upon his release from military prison and turned to drugs, which he became dependent on, leading to the beginning of his cycle of crime and incarceration.

SHANE: My father came out to visit me, and my girl-friend was also there. He said to me, in front of her, 'I don't want you to get out of the navy'. He expected me to go through this and still want to be a part of them after how they treated me. My father said, 'If you stay in the navy and you get rid of her, I'll give you $25,000 cash'. There was a big fucking argument. It blew me away, it was something I've never forgotten. I fucking said no, did the time, got out and stayed with her. He could see the writing on the wall but I couldn't.

She was young and still wanted to party and have a good time with her friends and go on her girlie nights out, me wanting to keep this family unit together and raise this family the best way I could. I wasn't happy with that: at the end of every week I'm sitting at home babysitting the child while she's out partying and having a good time.

That's where things started to break down. I found myself in a position where I had thrown away a career in the navy for this family, and this thing that I wanted to keep together was failing. Everywhere I turned I was failing. I was on my own again. I was at an all-time low. I had hit rock bottom, so I started to use drugs to cope with the stress and pressure and everything that was going on in my life, all the failings that I was experiencing. Before I knew it, this drug that I was experimenting with had become a partner; it was a security blanket, a comfort zone.

The only reason I did this crime was to keep her happy; all the money was spent on her, she was pressuring me for money. It was a pretty greedy thing on her behalf, and I ended up taking the rap for it. I only got caught because right at the end of it all, on the way home, we stopped off to fill the car up with petrol. Then—boom!—it was a federal charge because it was a stolen Bankcard I used. The federal police were looking for me.

That was basically where my fucking criminal activities began. First charge. After that all of it was related to drugs. As your body becomes more used to a drug you've got to spend $100 a day, then $200, [then] $300. You commit up to three offences a day: burglary, break and enter, stealing cars—basically stealing. It might start off as petty crime, then you might be picking up a weapon. It's a nomadic lifestyle when you're doing crime for drugs, because some weeks can be great and living in motels and having parties, and other times you can be destitute.

The next time I got caught, it was for break and enter offences, I think. I was given nine months [of] weekend detention but I never did a day of it. I decided that I wasn't going to take myself to jail on the weekend and I just didn't go. But eventually they picked me up for something and I got two years. That was the first time I went to jail.

For Michael and David, life became complicated early. Like his mum, by fifteen Michael was a parent, a responsibility he was not equipped to deal with.

MICHAEL: Just before I turned sixteen, my female friend gave birth to my daughter. She was at home with her mother and her sisters and I knew my daughter would be looked after. It wasn't really a concern to me, when it should have been. I think part of me wanted to go backwards because I knew I had responsibilities, I just didn't know how to handle it.

When I got a lot of money I would take things to my daughter, and even though she didn't know what they were I felt part of me was doing the right thing. That's what I thought responsibility was about. I wasn't actually sixteen yet, I still had six months to go.

I did try and settle down with [the woman who would become] my wife and went and lived with my mother, who had a flat at the time just across from where I first grew up. And my mother's boyfriend—my brother's father now—was in jail at that time ... so it was, like, Mum in one room, and me and my wife and my daughter in the other. I tried to be a family man but still only knew what I knew to do to get money and to get an income and support them, so it escalated to stolen cars. I used to come home every night, but [by] sunrise I'd be out doing jewellery stores and stuff.

David also became a father while still in his mid teens. The mother of his first child died while he was in jail.

DAVID: I met their mother when I was fourteen, in sixth class, we went to the same old school together. She was all right, she was a good girl but I think I tore her apart, you know, all the things I used to do. It just killed her. She got on the uppers and downers and she went to sleep and just didn't wake up. Happened when I first got this sentence. Because I got sentenced for twelve years on top and eight on the bottom, I just told her, 'Go and party on for a couple of years, don't worry about me, come and start visiting me four years later, go and have a life'. A couple of days later I found out she just didn't wake up. I didn't want to go to the funeral—I couldn't face the parents and shit like that.

AUTHOR: Were you planning to get married?

DAVID: There's a funny story to that, too, because when I had the child I was only a teenager. Well, she didn't tell me she was pregnant. I come home from school one day [and] my mum and dad said: 'Why don't you shower? We're going out for tea, it's just us going'. And I started saying 'Sucko' to my brothers, 'Sucko, see you later, sucko'. They were laughing at me a bit because me mum told them what was going on. I said, 'Where are we going?' 'We're going to your girl's house for tea.' I'm thinking I'll get a quickie there while my mum and dad's there—sex was on my mind all the time—so I went, 'Oh yeah, sweet'. I was grinning and that; pretty good, thought I was made. So we went down and her mum gave me the filthiest look, mate. My father and her father were sitting down and said, 'What's your plans?' I said, 'What do you mean?' because I didn't know what was going on. 'She's pregnant', they said. I went, 'What?' I spun right out when they said that, I started freaking out. I was stoned, had a couple of bongs with my brothers before I went, and I thought it was all a joke so I was spinning out. Then as soon as my dad talked I looked at him and he said, 'Yeah, Dave, you're having a son so you got to get married'. I went, 'Oh, yeah, wait, I'll just go to the toilet' and I jumped out the window and took off.

Then I started going into the city, and that's when the bashing happened and I went into the boys' home. And I remember getting out of the boys' home and all me brothers are in the car park and her mother and father and the boy—it's the first time I'd seen him. My father was at the exit with the car so I couldn't run again; he just grabbed me by the ear, pulled me in the back seat and started drumming me that I wasn't a kid. My dad used to say, 'Grow up, you're still young'. I said, 'Ah, it's all right, Dad, she'll be right, I know what I'm doing'. Mums and dads are always right in certain ways. My old man is a man of few words. I've always respected him, couldn't backchat him or nothing like that. Since I got locked up our parents had done the garages up in my house and her house—up like a granny flat. But I used to go out and party, go and visit me mates.

AUTHOR: Were you faithful to her?

DAVID: Always. Always.

AUTHOR: That was important to you.

DAVID: I couldn't even dream about doing nothing like that. We had a good relationship. She was a maddy, too, mate, she was a deadset glamour. She was an Aussie sheila, she had blondish–brownish hair, blue eyes; she was nice. Couldn't even think of playing up on her.

I used to go to parties with my mate and a lot of girls wanted to get me and I didn't want any part of it because mine was at home. My mum used to drum me: 'Don't muck up, Dave. How would you like it if your father mucked up on you?' Used to make me think.

AUTHOR: Half of you acted responsibly and half of you still wanted to play?

DAVID: Responsibility with her was, like, fifty-fifty. I used to do things for her. I used to let her go out with her friends and I used to babysit but used to have a couple of mates with me.

AUTHOR: How long were you out of the boys' home that time?

DAVID: Two months. I didn't last too long. I was pretty bad to her in that way. I admit I probably drilled away and that's how she got that way. But I've learnt a lot about myself. I can't change the past. Our eldest boy and that, you know, he's nothing like me; all the kids are like their mum—gentle.

As their violence and crimes became more serious, so too did the chance they would be caught. It was an inevitability that all these inmates faced, even though capture may well mean a prison sentence in an adult jail.

Getting Worse

Stuart was involved in an altercation over the loan of a guitar and ended up stabbing his former neighbour with a kitchen knife. He described what took place immediately following the incident.

STUART: I dropped the knife and I ran. I just ran and I went into shock and I was frightened, I was shaking. I ran out of the flat and I kept running and running. I ran about five kilometres. I eventually got to a place where I could make a phone call and I rang my parents. When I was coming home in the taxi, I come around the corner in my street and there were all these police cars at the front of my house.

They took me down to the local police station and put me in a holding cell and started asking me questions. I was in tears, I was shattered. I mean, I was that gone I couldn't smoke a cigarette, I couldn't answer questions.

And about four o'clock in the morning they gave me this fax sheet, saying, 'Do you realise that your mate is dead?' And I broke down again; I couldn't believe it. They said, 'We're going to arrest you for murder'. And the word 'murder' made me shiver. I was remanded in custody, too, and it took four days to realise I was in jail. I had never seen inside a jail cell.

I couldn't sleep. I started traumatising by seeing what I'd done, over and over and over and over again. Anyhow, as I got closer to people that had been in jail before and started getting their trust and, you know, understanding, I started to work everything out. Called my solicitor. Solicitor came down and eventually I got a psychological report and they released me on bail, so it was only thirty-eight days of incarceration that I spent.

My son was born in January the next year. My girlfriend was pregnant at the time the whole crime happened. I spent twenty-two months on bail before my trial came up. And the jury went out and come back with a verdict: 'Not guilty of murder but guilty of manslaughter'. And it hit me then.

For the majority of the inmates I spoke to, among their peer group jail was always a possible, even likely, eventuality. Having experienced incarceration in a milder form in boys' homes, it was something they were well aware of and would have preferred to avoid. However, knowing that they were destined for jail if they continued committing crimes did not mean that they had the maturity, determination and guidance to break their drug addictions and resolve their emotional problems and violent tendencies.

In the prisons that would be their destiny, the inmates would not learn appropriate social behaviour. Instead they learnt to adapt to their new environment and make the most of prison life.

Chapter 4:

Welcome to Prison

There were times during my visits to prison when I would be left alone waiting for an inmate to be called or an officer to let me out. I would take a moment to take in my surroundings in the cell or wing and imagine calling the place home. But no matter how much I had learnt from the inmates or the time I spent inside prison, I could not comprehend living there.

Inmates live in a world of locks. The drab walls, squeaky-clean linoleum floors and solid metal doors are cold, stark and instantly unwelcoming. Uniformed officers with keys dangling from heavy chains are firmly in control of every aspect of inmates' lives. And, if such living conditions are a lot to adjust to, there are also the fellow inmates to contend with.

No matter how menacing a person might have been on the streets, no-one enters prison without trepidation. And no matter what tales new inmates have heard from others or watched in movies about prison, nothing can really prepare them for the brutal reality of their new home.

The inmates I spoke with described prison as a micro-society in which survival required them to learn new life skills quickly. There were major adjustments to be made and little time to make them in.

SHANE: I was shit-scared. I still had this image of prison as what you see in the movies. I was delivered there by a truck and was put into a holding yard with about ten other guys who had all been there and done it before. Being a first-timer, I had to pick things up as quick as I could, and there's certain rules in jail that one must abide by. I did know one guy that I'd known on the street; he was an Aboriginal guy, real nice guy, and he gave me a quick run-down of what the go was; told me what to do, what not to do, what to say, what not to say, the things to turn my back on, the things not to turn my back on. He gave me some clothes so I didn't look like an idiot in the uniform they dress you up in, the basic green. They call it 'gronk gear'—it makes you look like a gronk. Through him I got to know other people, some of his friends. That's how the ball rolls and if you hook up with the right people, things start to go around. You've got to learn to fit in as quickly as possible or you can become a target. I probably was and looked as nervous as hell, but you've got to put on a front and toughen up real fast, show no emotions and put these barriers up and let nobody get in or at you.

STUART: You had a lot of worries because you didn't know what was true and what was false. You had to experience it for yourself, and every day was a new experience. Someone would say something to you and give you the insights and then you'd seen it for yourself and then they'd come back and say, 'Here's a perfect example'. So eventually, after eight months, I'd learnt heaps. The only problem was, I hadn't been in the main jail, it was only remand. And the way we were treated down in the remand—because you had your sweeper's job, this and that—we all got well looked after.
Some of the inmates that I was with had been in main jails and they told me, 'You have no idea what you are

Welcome to Prison
113

in for, because this is like Play School *at the moment. When you get to a main jail, you must learn all these little techniques of how to survive and how to get through a day and you'll do all right'.*

AUTHOR: When you were finally sent to prison proper, how was it walking into that cell the very first time?

STUART: It's very hard. You got to break the ice. It's very hard because you don't know the bloke you've moved in with but then you get put in with him and you got to work out each other. Can we get along? Are we going to be able to share things? But I was the sort of person that could communicate quite well and I got into that cell and the first night we had a long chat to the early hours. He probably wanted someone to talk to and I wanted to talk to him, and it was a bit comforting. But the next day, when you wake up in the morning, when they open the doors, they're going to be all new inmates, all new faces.

AUTHOR: Did you know anyone?

STUART: No. Not a soul. I think a good month went past before I was quite settled. Then one bloke comes up to me and says, 'You can work if you want to'. And he was making belts and was sending them home and he was putting some in the prison shop where they sell them in the art part and he was getting money for them. I thought, 'This is a good idea. When I get some money I can buy a television'. Because I had nothing then, I only had what I'd been incarcerated with and that was my clothes and cigarettes and a few letters.

Eventually you collect things. Inmates go home and they pass it on. You always got to put your hand up and say, 'I wouldn't mind that, leave that behind'. It's a process that all inmates know: when you go home, you leave behind everything as courtesy to another inmate that has nothing.

Having friends inside is a major advantage for anyone entering prison. Not only do they teach new inmates the rules for prison survival and offer clothes and other items, but, more importantly, they offer security, because in prison there is safety in numbers. Apart from Stuart and Jason, familiar faces greeted all the inmates upon their incarceration.

SHANE: When I got to Parramatta they put me in a double cell and they were six-out. When my mate and I walked in I saw four blokes I knew from the streets. One of me mates from our area was there, you know, and then the next morning I see half the people were from my area, all westies, you know; we knew these blokes.

DARREN: I think the first real jail sentence I got was twelve months or eighteen months. I would think I was scared at first, knowing that I had come into a place that is very unpredictable. [I had] heard a lot of stories, but once in there it wasn't as bad as what I thought it would've been, mainly because I had a lot of friends in there, friends from home.

AUTHOR: Did anyone try to test you?

DARREN: I would have been if I didn't have friends, most certainly; that would've been on the cards. But when people see that you know people inside, they go, 'Well, we can't really attack him because he's got back-up'. If you got to a jail where you know basically nobody, you are in trouble.

David and Michael told me that for them, as Aboriginal Australian inmates, meeting a friend or relative in prison is no surprise; it's like a neighbourhood reunion.

DAVID: I didn't care if I would end up in jail because all me friends were in jail. This is the '80s and everyone from Waterloo or Redfern was in jail, so I didn't care if I went in there because I would know everybody. When I come to jail I had so many mates here, I loved it. I was scared at first, don't get me wrong, everybody's first time is scary. But then a couple of my brother's friends come up to me and made me feel more comfortable, then my brother got transferred from his jail to where I was and he was there with me. He was doing seven years and he'd done three of them, so he knew everybody in the system and got me to know everybody—told me who to be careful with and who not to be careful with, who to respect and who not to respect, just taught me the ways of jail. It's just one big learning experience, and the strong, they're the ones that survive out here and the weak go out in body bags.

MICHAEL: I suppose in a way I'd hoped that it wasn't going to happen. My uncles have been in prison and some of them had told me what it's like, and one of them was saying, 'Hey, you'll be right, you'll be right' and the other one was trying to scare me, 'Listen, they'll try and sodomise you'.

I remember sitting in the police cells for ... twenty-one days ... and that whole three weeks I was scared and I was nervous 'cause it was unexpected, nothing I knew. I wasn't literally shitting myself but I was scared.

AUTHOR: How did you prepare yourself for prison?

MICHAEL: I knew that my best friend was there and I knew what reputation he had in prison and I thought I'd use that as a positive, to conquer the fear as much as I could.

I remember we got here at about ten o'clock, eleven o'clock in the morning and didn't get into the wing until night-time. There was about fifteen of us and that was when I was the most fearful, there and then, 'cause I was actually inside the jail and it was like, 'All right, this is the go'.

They walked us over to the wing and we got up on the top landing and, bang, I'd seen the boys and that. They were over in the other wing but I'd seen some that I knew. Went in the cell and it was just like, whoa, this is where we live. And I didn't feel as fearful, because I was with people that I knew and trusted to an extent and I knew that in the morning I was going to see a lot more friends and my best friend and family members and all that who were in the other wing. So I was sort of laid-back. There's safety in knowing that I have protection, so to speak. If anything happens, I know that they're going to stand up and not let it happen and try and prevent it as best they can.

AUTHOR: How did it compare to the boys' homes?

MICHAEL: In the boys' homes I was told what to do. I was told to mop my cell—my room—vacuum it, make sure that my bed was all made properly, no creases in the thing, no hairs in the shower, or I'd lose points, I'd lose time off visits and I'd lose activities like swimming in the pool. Even though I was old enough to smoke cigarettes, I was still only allowed to have six a day. It was like I was a child in the boys' home.

But then when you come to jail it was, like, whoa. Like, in a jail they're called officers and in the boys' home they're called youth workers. And the prison officers just stay down there and they don't come near you, whereas the youth officers are in your face all day telling you to do this and that, and it was, like, a big turnaround for me. I was thinking to myself, 'Fuck, this is mad, this is excellent'.

Inmates with the right friends can while away their sentences high on drugs. Although supply is irregular, all drugs are widely available but expensive. For obvious reasons the inmates divulged few details on their current drug use, but I sensed that at least a couple of them smoked marijuana shortly before I interviewed them.

MICHAEL: I hadn't been sentenced yet so I kicked back and I had a cup of tea and I smoked drugs—there was heaps of drugs—and I thought, this isn't even work, being locked up. It wasn't what I expected jail to be.

The only thing that was wrong is that I didn't have good clothes and that but the boys helped me out and I knew I'd get more help the next day with clothes and that.

The public's perception, driven by sensationalist stories in the media, is that life in jail is comfortable, even resort-like: three meals a day, colour television, laundry facilities, just like a hotel. But while hotels are built for comfort, older prisons such as Long Bay were based on the punitively inspired British designs. Walking into a prison cell—where inmates are locked in for upwards of fourteen hours a day— I was struck by the lack of space. Besides the double bunk, open metal toilet and washbasin, actual living space is non-existent. Shane provided an analogy during one of our conversations: he told me that if I wanted a realistic idea of what it's like to call a prison cell home I should take a single mattress with me and move into my bathroom for a weekend—then I should imagine having to share the space with a complete stranger who may not shower for days, listens to the radio too loudly or is just unpleasant company.

When my curiosity got the better of me I did ask about in-cell toilet etiquette; I learnt that there is an unspoken agreement among inmates to make an effort to use the facilities elsewhere in the wing before being locked in for the night.

On one occasion an officer left me in a cell that had been converted into a makeshift office and went off to get the inmate that I was set to interview. With a minute or so to myself, I swung the steel door shut and sat on one of the two plastic chairs which, along with a basic and bare desk, were the cell's only furniture. Within a few seconds I felt claustrophobic—a sensation I'm not prone to experience. Just entertaining the thought of such confinement, imagining what it would be like in reality, was almost impossible to grasp. I asked Jason for his thoughts on the lack of space.

JASON: I'm a bit of a loner, so I like my own personal space so I can do what I want when I want without having to be considerate of other people. But in jail there's someone always in your face, you've got no privacy. Like, you've got a toilet in your cell and when you have to go, you have to go. And when people have just come to jail they've got no consideration because a lot of them have just been living with their mummy or had their girlfriend picking up after them and they're very inconsiderate and hard to live with. It's very frustrating. If you're asleep they'll be coming in and out waking you up and that's really annoying. Long-termers are usually more considerate, they'll try and be quiet if you're asleep.

AUTHOR: Other inmates have told me that when new inmates first arrive in prison they don't appreciate the value of privacy and tend to be in your face.

JASON: New ones are always asking questions, and that pissed me off after a while, especially if they're only saying it for conversation. That can get very frustrating. I always find that when I'm two-out with somebody, after a while little things piss me off, really start to get to me. You try and be as tolerant as you can. That's the thing about jail—it teaches you patience.

I actually just got a new cellmate yesterday and he snores. Drives me crazy because I'm a light sleeper. But you can go to the office and tell them, 'I want to move in with one of your [my] friends', and usually *they'll let you. If they like you they'll let you. Or you just tell your cellmate, 'Look, this isn't working out' and ask him to move.*

That prison is about the denial of liberty is something all inmates are acutely aware of; the sense of confinement is everywhere, manifested by locks, gates, doors and security cameras. I asked the inmates how they dealt with these constant reminders of their lack of freedom—especially the clanging noise of the gates slamming. All said that they became less sensitive towards it and that the evidence of their confinement became a norm in their lives, fading into the background. But as Gordon pointed out to me, 'you're always somewhat aware, otherwise you've become institutionalised'.

SHANE: I hate prison. Prison is a shit-hole. All the blokes I know don't want to come back to jail. The biggest thing is the freedom; the basic things like being able to go to the beach on a weekend, have sex with your girlfriend, go to the pub and have a beer, go for a drive down the coast, go to the shop and buy a can of Coke. Not just on a Tuesday at eleven o'clock when it suits them.

Of all the inmates I interviewed, only Michael spoke candidly about women, or the lack thereof. One can only surmise that lack of sexual activity is a major issue for inmates but not a topic that men, particularly those with such traditional views on masculinity, are willing to discuss. I asked Michael what he missed most from the outside world.

MICHAEL: No sex.

AUTHOR: What about the loss of freedom; for example, going to the beach?

MICHAEL: I think freedom would be very close to sex but sex takes the cake. Then there's, like, the freedom of walking down to the shop and buying an ice-cream. I miss walking down the street and buying an ice–cream and I miss taking my kids to the park and pushing them on a swing. I miss going over to my father's house or my grandmother's house and having a cup of tea and a cigarette with them. Just little things in life. I miss having a bath, mate.

Inmates consider their cells their homes, both physically and emotionally. Several said that it was only once they were locked in for the night that they could truly relax. Within their small confines inmates go to great length to personalise their space with trinkets, photographs and permitted household basics like a kettle, hotplate, radio or television. They attempt to give the cold stark walls a sense of homeliness, in essence creating something to take pride in. But in prison, 'home' is a very disrupted concept. Searches for contraband—cells being turned inside out— are a regular occurrence.

When I arrived one morning for an interview, Shane seemed agitated following a search of his cell the night before.

SHANE: Like, I had a bit of [a] run-in last week. They decided to be arseholes and went through my cell, just to raise the pressure a bit for me. That's my home, that's where I live. I work my arse off in here, I do the right thing, I've been in no trouble, I don't use drugs, I play the game, I respect them, and they went out of their way just to let me know I'm still in jail and that they're in charge.

Prisoners are also often moved around the system, meaning that whatever social contacts or stability they enjoyed can be instantly disrupted. It also means that any scams they might be benefiting from have to be abandoned. These might include a more comfortable cell or obtaining an extra ration of milk from a mate in the kitchen, to more elaborate schemes such as standover tactics and drug running. The move from one facility to another can occur without warning.

JASON: I've been to probably around ten different prisons. I hated it because you've got to start again, making new friends. You've got your little rorts on the side where you might get a carton of milk off this bloke, and when you go to a new jail you have to start again. But it doesn't take long. Now I could go to any jail and know at least five people.

After Stuart had adjusted to life in Lithgow jail, he was told to prepare his things for a move.

STUART: They come up to me and said, 'You're going on an escort'. And the problem was that I was settled and I was quite happy there. I said to them, 'Where are we going?', and they said, 'We're going back to the remand centre first on transit but you'll be going north to Grafton'. And I thought, 'I just got settled in this jail, now I've got to go back to another one'. So I said my goodbyes. It's hard to leave friends behind, because you get acquainted with people and it's like the only family you got, and then when you walk away from them you know that you'll probably never ever see them again. Never. You know their stories, their life. If you're on the outside, then you'd probably have a beer with this bloke.

I moved on to Grafton, and you've got to break that wall down again, you've got to find a routine. You have no idea how long you're going to be there. I liked to work, because I knew I had to work to keep that time kicking over and my mind occupied. I eventually got into a routine and did some education up there when I could, because there wasn't really much available. I did some 'conflict resolution' sort of class. Because it was a small jail it only had limited opportunities. If you didn't work, you were just put out in the yard all day, you weren't paid … you were just given the minimum rate. Sit around, smoke cigarettes, drink coffee all day or get bored and get in trouble.

Some prisons run industries, offering inmates the ability to work and earn money to spend in the prison shop. These industries are spread across the state and include outside contracts like a nursery, sawmill, metal workshop and even assembling and packing airline headphones. Some industries supply the prison itself, including a dairy, bakery and farm produce. Inmates may spend up to $50 at the weekly buy-up, with goods being pre-ordered and the funds taken out of the inmates' prison account. The buy-up is essentially a basic grocery store, selling foodstuffs such as biscuits, chips, jam as well as cigarettes or tobacco and toiletries. Bigger ticket items such as a television, toaster or sneakers can be ordered by special request.

STUART: Some mornings we woke up and we didn't want to go to work. But we knew we had to go to work because we had to kill a day. I knew that sitting in that yard for six-and-a-half hours was going to kill me. So when I went to jail, the first thing I said to myself was: 'I'll work at every opportunity that I can. If I can't work, I'll just study and keep my mind occupied'.

Eventually I was moved again. I was going to an area near where my family lived, and I hadn't seen them for six months. The only contact was by mail or phone call and I wanted to see them in person ... I hadn't seen my son for at least seven months. We got to the remand centre and I sat there for about two or three days, [was] put on a truck and come to Long Bay. It was all new to me again but the inmate that was with me had been in jail for the last six years, so he knew a few people.

The only way I've seen Long Bay was from the outside. Now I was going to see the inside. What did I expect? I'd heard bad rumours about Long Bay.

I came into the ten-wing [Wing Ten], which is like the reception wing for people who are doing programs. Anyway, here I am and I've got to break the ice again. You get nervous because people don't know who you are. And eventually, a couple of days later, I had spoken to about ten blokes. I didn't know them all but at least I knew that I could go to their cell and have a chat to them and ask them something or this and that. And eventually I moved into here and I've been here ever since.

Inmates in maximum-security prisons are locked inside their cells following an early dinner in the mid-afternoon, and their doors are not opened again until the following morning.

STUART: You get used to it eventually. When you first get locked in at 3.30 you say, 'How will I deal with it? I'm not even coming home from school at that time'. Here you are, 3.30, you're locked in a cell and you can't go anywhere—it's like your mother used to confine you to your room.

I was in a corner cell, which can have three people. You have a shower [in the cell], you got your toilet and that. And you all have to get on. One bloke I came from Lithgow with, and the old bloke we just met when I was at the remand centre. So we were already acquainted with each other a bit and we got on together. So it was a family now. One wants to paint, the other one wants to write letters or one wants to watch television. So you all adapt. Everybody adapts. We all tried to help each other with routine.

Adjusting to prison life is a challenge for the sane, but for those inmates with a mental illness things are far more complicated. The number of inmates with a history of mental illness is very high—a study by the Department of Corrective Services in 2002 found that one-third of new inmates have had contact with mental health services in the six months prior to being arrested.[24] Such has been the case since the closure of public psychiatric hospitals in the 1980s in favour of supervised housing that never materialised. The result has been that many mentally ill patients are left to fend for themselves, and invariably some end up in prison, only exacerbating their mental instability.

Away from their family and friends and thrown into a hostile environment, those who are emotionally vulnerable, depressed or fearful may become despondent and attempt suicide. In 2002 almost 2000 inmates in NSW prisons were either identified as being at risk of self-harm or attempted suicide.[25]

Jason was incarcerated for the unprovoked murder of his flatmate in a frenzied knife attack. He was prescribed psychiatric medication, which he stored away, using them to overdose while in remand awaiting his court case.

JASON: At first I was on remand waiting for my court case, which was really frustrating because you don't move on, you don't know what you're looking at. Plus I wasn't working, so I had a lot of time on my hands; I was always playing cards and it gets pretty boring after a while.

When I first came into jail, their answer was, 'Let's load him full of pills so he can't harm anyone or harm himself'. They tried to, but I didn't really take them; I'd take one here and there and that was it. I ended up saving them all up. Actually, I ended up trying to commit suicide. I took about 150 different psych pills that I'd saved up and that other people had given me, and through that I ended up having two cardiacs and a lung collapse. I was pretty lucky I never died. About three times I tried to kill myself while I was on remand. I thought, 'Well, I'm only a young fellow in jail for murder'. I thought I was going to spend the rest of my life in jail and I really didn't want that. I was on remand for fifteen months, and that's a long time to be in limbo. So my stress levels were way up and I found it really hard. I thought, 'Nah, prison is not the life I want to live'. So that was my answer, but obviously God had other plans for me.

The thing that snapped me out of trying it again was one of my mates. He said, 'You know, you're really selfish, you don't think about anyone but yourself. How do you think your sister would feel?' Because my sister was coming in every week and she was very supportive. He said, 'How do you think she would feel if you took your life?' And I never thought about it [like that] and it was like a slap in the face and that sort of snapped me out of it and made me think of the consequences. Since then I've never tried again. I'm embarrassed about it a bit. It's not something I'm proud of. But I really did want to die; I was spewing when I woke up.

AUTHOR: Did they give you psychiatric care when you came in?

JASON: They did, and I was seeing quite a few psychiatrists and some of them have got more problems than the people inside. The first guy I'd ever seen, he had a nervous tic, his neck was going to one side and I started laughing at him. And he said, 'What are you laughing at?', and I said, 'Nothing', and he wrote down that I was a schizo because I was laughing at nothing, but I was laughing at him and I couldn't tell him that. A lot of them shouldn't be working in here.

A private psychiatrist backed me for diminished responsibility in court, so when I got sentenced I was relieved. 'I sentence you to nine years with an additional term of five years', and that was just a big relief, a big weight off my shoulders, because I was thinking twenty years. Even nine years is a long time but with my fifteen months backdated I had seven and a half to go and I thought, 'Well I'll have a go and see how I go'.

During my time conducting interviews in prison, I asked each inmate for any advice they would give to new inmates.

What would they tell me, for example, if I were about to begin a prison sentence?

JASON: Just keep to yourself, be yourself, don't try to be someone you're not, don't try and impress people, and mind your own business. That's my advice. And stay away from drugs and gambling. That's probably one of wisest things someone said to me when I first come in: he said, 'If you want to do your time a lot easier, stay away from the drugs and the gambling', which is true. If you end up getting a habit you'll find it really hard in jail. It's just too expensive. That's one thing I have seen a lot of since I've been in jail. You've got the mainstream in here and you've got protection. Well, a lot of blokes will get themselves in debt through gambling or drugs and they end up going to protection because they can't pay, and [they] end up getting bashed.

Darren had witnessed this from close range, as both a customer and a supplier.

DARREN: In jail there's little lurks and perks or there's little deals to be made, there's little avenues that you go on. You don't have to be smart to get off on drugs all the time, you've just got to know the right people, say, 'Yeah, mate, I can sell a bit of that', and you're in, if they trust you.

   I've sold a lot of drugs in jail to certain nationalities and it's worked out for me. But I never had to hurt anyone over the money. I've warned their missus when they're talking on the phone and that, said, 'If you don't bring me $50 on a visit in two weeks, your *boyfriend's going to have problems'. But I'll give them two weeks where other people only give two or three days. I don't expect it straightaway; they're not going anywhere, mate. So within two weeks surely she'd give it to the boyfriend and he'd come and give it to me. If they don't bring it, I'll go and talk to my people and someone else will come and deal with you; I don't want to know about it.*

AUTHOR: Do people get killed over it?

DARREN: That's most certainly common. People get stabbed over it. People will book $400 or $500 worth of heroin and then go into protection, 'I'm not paying that'. If they stay at the main they're going to get stabbed. I had a mate who got stabbed twenty-seven times in the back and now he's paraplegic.

Inmates who are housed in a facility where no work is available receive a weekly allowance of $12.70, which is credited to their prison account. More than 60 per cent of inmates are employed in prison industries and can earn up to $63.90 each week.[26]

DARREN: In here, $20 to me is a lot of money. I don't get money sent in, so what I earn I've got to live off. Next week I'll get some money when me mum comes. That money helps me get a ciggie packet a week or anything like that. I don't say 'Give us the money or I'll kick your guts in, Mum'. Most people do that— threaten their families. Or, 'You bitch, why don't you get in here, what are you doing?' And it's not their fault you're here, it's your fault. My mum is straight-

up. I said to her once, 'Mum, I need $100 because I got into a bit of trouble'. She said, 'Pay your own way, I ain't paying shit'. So I had to go back and try to negotiate with the bloke, give him something, TV or whatever. A lot of people get themselves in trouble this way, a hell of a lot of them do. It's all for drugs.

Inmates who are not granted bail or those awaiting transfer to more permanent accommodation are held in remand. Here, a mix of inmates charged with a variety of crimes and at different stages of their court cases or imprisonments live in a tense and uncertain environment with a fast inmate turnaround and heightened emotions.

Stuart, during his lengthy stay in the remand centre, was fortunate to land the job of a sweeper. Every prison wing has a sweeper, a position that offers small concessions of freedom and is therefore coveted by inmates. Appointed for their trustworthiness and acceptance by the other inmates, the position does involve actual sweeping duties, along with various other liaison tasks within the wing. Sweepers are paid for their services, have access around the wing not available to regular inmates and they spend more hours outside their cells. Stuart's job included showing new arrivals the ropes.

STUART: We used to have a meeting every morning with the new remand inmates, blokes that had never been in jail before. We had to explain to them the rules so they wouldn't get themselves in trouble—if they needed anything this is who they had to approach. See, some of the blokes come in there and they didn't even know how to get a toothbrush or how to fill out a form or what process they should do. Even though they were in trouble and even though they've done a bad thing, at least they got some sort of idea of what they were going to have to do to get through. But then they get into the routine and they understand what happens.

AUTHOR: You were pretty lucky to be made sweeper—I imagine that your self-esteem was given a boost pretty well straightaway.

STUART: My mind was being occupied by what I could give to the other inmates. The only thing they can think of is anger. They're angry at what's happened. They're angry at everybody. And this causes the little altercations, maybe with officers, maybe with other inmates. And we prepared them for the hard road. It might be a long road, they may not see their family again for a long time, and they were preparing themselves for that.

When discussing the rules of prison life, all the inmates stressed one as being the most important of all—don't get involved.

STUART: Well, if something happens, [if] an inmate does something wrong—say, he steals something off another inmate—and you see it, you cannot say anything about it, okay? Because if you say something, what you're doing is you're being like a witness and it's what they call a 'dog' in jail. And being called a 'dog' in jail is the most awful thing to be.

AUTHOR: Is it a death sentence?

STUART: It can be. If someone ... gives evidence against you in crime and they're also incarcerated for the crime, they got to go on protection. That was a crime against a criminal and the ultimate punishment is death. And the only way to get away from that was to go on protection—to go into another category of inmates that don't come into mainstream.

JASON: The worst one I ever saw was at Goulburn. In the yard there were twenty blokes standing around, and all of a sudden this one bloke who had a bat, he'd hit this bloke in the mouth and the whole twenty of them just jumped in, kicking him. But apparently he told on somebody so that's the price he had to pay, especially in that prison.

Gordon, the most experienced of the inmates, succinctly offered his advice to new inmates.

GORDON: Keep your head down. Don't go standing out in the crowd.

AUTHOR: What does 'do your own time' mean?

GORDON: Well, if you bring your problems to me, right? And you're downloading on me a lot of things that are happening to you outside or inside, right? If you've got problems inside you just do your own time.

The kind of society prison inmates live in was of greater interest to me than their physical environment. In order to adapt to prison life, the inmates had to adopt an assertive and fearless persona, disguise any vulnerability they felt and use violence as the central means of resolving conflict and imposing superiority.

Chapter 5:
Living in the Jungle

Most of us have a perception of prison as a violent place. Overwhelmingly this violence is perpetrated by inmates against each other, rather than by prison officers. The threat of violence is an ever-present element of prison life. Prison society is somewhat Darwinian, operating on the principle of survival of the fittest. This is particularly so in maximum-security facilities, where inmates are more violent, movement and freedom are controlled to a large degree and inmates may feel they have far less to lose.

The level of violence is also related to ovecrowding, which is not uncommon considering the phenomenal increase in the rate of convictions and length of sentences handed down over the past decade.[27] In 1962, *Scientific American* published the results of a now often quoted population density study by psychologist John Calhoun. In a laboratory he placed rats in increasingly congested housing then observed and recorded what happened. He noted that among the male rats, aggressive behaviour, withdrawal, cannibalism and violent sexual encounters were clear consequences of a reduction in personal space.[28]

In prison, muscle—real or perceived—equals status. It is a society in which any signs of emotion or vulnerability are instantly recognised as weaknesses to be exploited. As we saw in the previous chapter, new inmates must quickly learn to adopt a confident facade of overt and old-fashioned masculinity. They must be prepared to demonstrate an ability and determination to fight, because predators loom in every wing.

The harrowing slices of life that the inmates share in this chapter are not dissimilar to patterns of behaviour found among animals, where the weak and vulnerable ultimately face demise.

While conducting these interviews, I was frequently asked by friends and acquaintances about the advent, or otherwise, of rape in prison. According to the number of complaints made, prison rape is a rare occurrence. This, however, should surprise no-one, considering that for inmates, implicating another inmate before officers or the law is the equivalent of a death sentence. 'Dogs'—those who inform on fellow inmates—sit at the bottom of prison hierarchy, not far from the most despised of inmates, paedophiles, otherwise known as 'rock spiders'. Prison culture also relegates rapists to lower status, but murderers— particularly whose victims were figures of authority such as policemen—are afforded the highest status.

Rape is part and parcel of prison culture. Increasingly, magistrates and judges take this into consideration when pronouncing sentences, particularly on those who are young and of slight build. in 1991, the then Minister for Corrective Services, Michael Yabsley, responded to a reporter's question on whether rape is inevitable in jail by stating, 'Regrettably, yes. I would be foolish to suggest otherwise'.[29]

The incidence of sexual assault in prison is a difficult problem to fully gauge. In a story that appeared in *The Age* in July 2001, journalist Bill Birnbauer asked a spokesperson for the Victorian Department of Human Services about prison rape.[30] The spokesperson denied that a problem existed, saying that only two cases of sexual assault have been confirmed in the past decade. However, In 1998 magistrate David Heilpern investigated this subject, conducting the most comprehensive survey of its kind in Australia, based on anonymous questionnaires and in-depth interviews with inmates. Heilpern found that one-quarter of all inmates have been sexually assaulted while in custody.[31] Realistically, if you are young, small in stature, and have no friends inside, you can expect the worst.

Prison rape is less about the sexual gratification of the perpetrators—who don't regard themselves as being homosexual—and more about empowerment, intimidation, humiliation and subjugation. 'Standing over' is an expression I heard frequently while inside prisons, and it occurs every moment of every day in many ways, with rape being its worst manifestation.

On one occasion I was given a tour around several wings neighbouring the VPP. The officer conducting the tour explained to me that when a vulnerable-looking inmate enters prison they are offered accommodation in protective custody—what inmates call 'the boneyard'. But entering protection is not an easy decision for an inmate to make— while these facilities offer greater supervision and safety, they also severely curtail an inmate's movements and employment and educational opportunities. Even more significant for those serving longer sentences is the knowledge that once in protective custody there is, by and large, no going back into the general population. Such inmates have already been branded as weak and become targets wherever they go. Worst of all, the inmates told me, is the experience of those inmates who become targets within protective custody.

Towards the end of the visit, the officer took me to a single-storey building set on a neatly trimmed lawn. It was eerily quiet and still in the Kevin Waller Unit for inmates at risk of suicide (part of the Malabar Special

Programs Centre). From the central recreation area a corridor stretched towards one end of the building lined with cells on either side; the cells were empty except for a mattress, book or magazine and a surveillance camera. Each housed an inmate on suicide watch, curled in the foetal position, unmoving. All were young, small in stature and appeared lifeless. So disturbed were they by their recent experiences that our invasive presence did not seem to even register. These inmates had suffered the worst of what prison has to offer.

> JASON: When I first came to jail what scared me was that if you show emotion, people see that as weakness. And in here you can smell fear and you can see it by body language; you can just sense it. I can sense it now if someone is scared, straightaway. When I first came in they put a bloke with me who was serving seven days for a fine. I'm ready to go up on a charge of murder and he's in for a seven-day fine. I told him what I was in for and he freaked straightaway and said, 'You're not going to kill me, are you?' And I tried to explain, 'Well, I'm not like that. It was just one minute of madness. It's not as if I do that day by day'.

This once common punishment of imprisoning traffic offenders who fail to pay their fines was amended following the much-publicised assault on eighteen-year-old Jamie Partlic in 1987.[32] While serving a one-day sentence, for failing to pay traffic fines, in a maximum-security prison wing, Partlic was attacked by several inmates. He was left in a coma for two months and sustained permanent brain injuries. One of the inmates relayed to me matter-of-factly that Partlic was merely resisting potential rapists.

AUTHOR: Did anyone test you?

JASON: I had one particular thing when I'd only just came to jail. I was a young twenty-eight-year-old fresh off the street and I was scared because you hear all the stories of rape. I was only fifty-eight kilos, so I was pretty skinny and that made me a bit of a target. One night I was asleep and I woke up and my cellmate was rubbing me up [so] I just jumped up swinging. It was three in the morning and we're fighting in this area four-foot wide, and I was shitting myself because I thought he was going to rape me. But then it was over and we stopped fighting. No-one really won. The next day I went up to the office and said, 'Move me'. They said, 'Why?', and I said, 'Just move me'. And because I wouldn't tell them what for they wouldn't move me. I had a black eye and he had a cut on his head so it was pretty obvious we were both fighting. So I ended up staying with him for another two weeks and I was starting to spin out, thinking he might try and rape me. But later he apologised. He said, 'I thought you were like that', so I calmed down.

AUTHOR: Have you known other people it's happened to?

JASON: I remember there was one bloke I came across—he'd been raped by six people and was a mess, wouldn't talk to people, was in his own little world. They totally messed him up. I haven't heard of it that much lately, but I have heard of people getting stood over. A few blokes will say, 'Either give us a head job or we'll bash you and rape you'.

I've seen a few things, like blokes get stabbed, which always gives me butterflies. I feel sorry for the person that's copping it and I suppose it's scary. That's in maximum-security, where there really is a lot of tension in the air, you can feel it; especially around Christmas there's a lot of fights. And Goulburn especially is a very violent jail. Two of my friends ended up getting stabbed ten times each in the showers [there].

AUTHOR: Why is it so violent?

JASON: Anger is the big emotion in jail. A lot of people are angry. A lot of people in jail still don't take responsibility for their own actions and are caught up in blaming everyone else, so they've got a lot of anger towards society. It's probably a lot of different emotions spilling into one and anger is the end result. One thing you learn is that you've got to stand up for yourself in here, you can't lay down, because once people see that you're a target then everyone will jump on the bandwagon and you'll be a target for everybody. They reckon humans are the most adaptable creatures; you just adapt to it and become numb to it. Time does it. You block it out. Jail really makes you block out a lot of your emotions, so that's where I'm finding trouble now: I want my emotions back but I'm finding it hard to find a lot of them because I pushed them down for so long.

I probably had a lot less confrontation with people because of my crime; [it] probably made people a little bit hesitant or wary, which I never played on, which is good. But I've seen it so often, where people's cell-mates will really play on it and go out of their way to scare them. They use fear to survive here. They intimidate people, stand over them for their smokes and use fear to get people to do things for them—maybe bring drugs in and that. But I know what it's like being scared and I don't like being scared and I wouldn't want to do that [to] someone else. I'd try and make them feel comfortable, I try to cut their fear down before it's started because I realised that fear makes people really unpredictable, and people do things they normally wouldn't do when they're scared. You don't know—maybe they might be working it up in their head and you end up with a shiv sticking in your back.

I had a situation one time where a bloke came up to me and he was going, 'Why have you been talking about me?' And I'm, 'I've never seen you before'. I stood up and he hit me and I hit him back, so they threw me in segro, and when I got out the next day he came up behind me and started on again. For me it's always been situations where someone else started it for me. But I've only had six fights since I've been here, so that's not too bad. And since my attitude has changed in the last three, four years I haven't had a fight, so that's pretty good.

STUART: When you see these things you get a bit of a fright yourself because you know it's there in spirit, within the inmates. You know that they're quite capable of doing anything. They could break at any minute and you could be the subject of the problem. And you sometimes think: how would I deal with it? And I think you just have to make a decision when it happens, you know? But you don't go there.

AUTHOR: Did anyone test you?

STUART: Oh, yeah, blokes pestering me. They seek it out, you know? Sometimes you go to a buy-up shop and you say no to somebody and they get offensive. And they don't like it because they've been told no. And they try and stand over you, and you take it as far as you have to, you know—you've got to fight for your rights.

AUTHOR: You must see some people come in and you think they're not going to last?

STUART: I seen it in the remand centre. I said, 'They won't last five days'. I seen a bloke, all he did was cry. I said to him, 'You don't cry in jail'. But he was crying because his mental state made him cry and his self-esteem must have been that low.

AUTHOR: But that doesn't elicit sympathy in here.

STUART: It gave us a bit of sympathy because we knew that he couldn't handle himself. So we looked out for him. He got upset one night, wanted to hang himself. And I said, 'Don't even say it. Don't even mention that you want to hang yourself, because they will take you away and there's nothing we can do about it'. I said, 'You've just got to hang in there'. And before we'd go to bed we just make sure he was all right, watching the television and this and that, and he got through and he lasted about three weeks there.

Even if inmates are not subjected to sexual assault themselves, they cannot help but see and hear it happen around them. I was interested to learn how they contend with hearing cries in the night from the next cell or seeing brutality inflicted on others? The answer is to develop a self-preserving immunity to what is normal behaviour in their society.

> SHANE: The jail culture is hear no, see no, speak no evil. The basic rules that you learn [are]: you don't tell on people, you do your own thing and you don't get yourself into positions that you can't get yourself out of. The culture is that you've got to look out for yourself. I don't get involved in other people's business. You have to just block it out and thank your lucky stars it's not happening to you. I mean, no-one wants to see a bloke get bashed to [a] pulp in a corner and you feel helpless but there's nothing you can do to help the guy.
>
> You can't let people disrespect you in front of other people in here. It makes you a weak person and every Tom, Dick and Harry is hanging shit on you if they think you're a weak person, 'He's a piece of shit, you can just put shit on him'. People that are weak and vulnerable and [have] never been to jail before stand out. It's like having fifteen footy players in one group and having a synchronised swimmer standing next to them. It's that blatantly obvious to everybody.

I put to Shane something I had read in a book by Primo Levi. Levi was a Holocaust survivor and later became an articulate voice for those who survived the experience. In *The Drowned and the Saved*, Levi distinguished the two forms of violence he witnessed while a prisoner in the Auschwitz concentration camp—'useful' violence used to achieve an end, and 'useless violence' inflicted for its own sake.[33]

SHANE: It's useless violence. It's just to stamp their authority, make themselves … a tough guy in the jail. People do it for self-satisfaction. It makes them feel good to be able to strut [around] the yard and kick someone's face in. A person could ask this new kid for a smoke and they say, 'No, I don't smoke' and the next time he walks past he kicks his face in because he hasn't got a smoke. It turns my gut. I've seen it happen that many times, day in day out, day after day after day.

AUTHOR: Can you relax in jail?

SHANE: You're always tense, especially in maximum-security because that's where it all happens, all the violence. Some jails are worse than others but you can never ever lose sight that anything can happen to anyone at any time. The place may be running like a clock then it might just take someone saying the wrong thing and there's an explosion, there's violence. You've got to be aware the whole time.

DARREN: If there's any jail I'd rather be in it'd be Lithgow. That's my jail of choice. It's just a beautiful jail. It's heavy but it's not. There's work there, there's a lot to do there, you know where you stand with certain people. Here it's very unpredictable— you just look at someone or stare at them and you're in trouble, mate.
   But don't worry, I'll walk around in all jails on edge, very tense, knowing that I haven't said anything about anyone or haven't done anything. It's the atmosphere. You can't be naive, like, 'It's not going to happen to me

because I haven't done anything wrong'. You don't have to do anything wrong, it just comes to you. If you're not prepared to stand up they will just milk you every chance that they get. I've been with blokes that have walked up to other people and have gone, 'I want $500 in my account tomorrow or you're a dead man'. I don't ask for trouble, I didn't look for it, I don't associate with them kind of people anymore.

I used to love the jail politics, love them, but [now] I just want to go home. It was good when you'd walk in with two or three mates and you know that you're the man basically and nothing is going to happen to you because you've got backup. You can take whatever you want and they're not going to say nothing to the screws. But if the man jumped up and showed a bit of heart, he'll be left alone.

AUTHOR: Have you ever been stood over?

DARREN: At Maitland jail someone come in and took my TV but I soon got it back. I said, 'If you don't put it back things are going to happen, mate'. He said, 'What are you going to do if I smack you in the mouth?' I said, 'I won't be standing there, mate, we will be going hammer and tong'. And I had the most well-respected bloke in the New South Wales [prison] system back down. And for someone like that to grab me and put me under their wing was a load off my mind. People wouldn't say anything to me then, they wouldn't stab me because they knew if they did they'd have trouble.

AUTHOR: Have you ever stood over anyone?

Malabar Special Programs Centre,
Long Bay Correctional Complex, Sydney

Shane: I don't agree with the outside mentality of lock us up
and throw away the key. What people aren't thinking is: what
about when we get released? They want to lock us up and treat
us like animals but when we get out we'll still act like animals.

Wing Ten Malabar Special Programs Centre:
a maximum-security facility that has an atmosphere
considerably tenser than that of the nearby Violence
Prevention Program, where the interviews were conducted.

That prison is about the denial of liberty is something
all inmates are acutely aware of; the sense of confinement
is everywhere, manifested by locks, gates, doors and
security cameras.

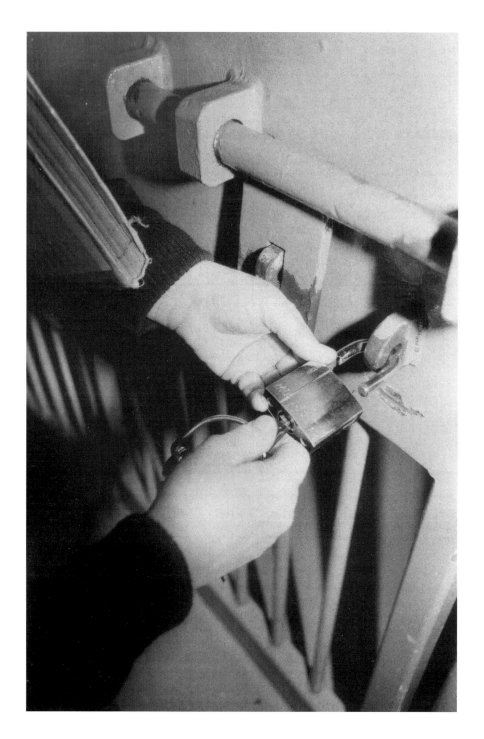

Inmates live in a world of locks. The drab walls, squeaky-clean linoleum floors and solid metal doors are cold, stark and instantly unwelcoming. Uniformed officers with keys dangling from heavy chains are firmly in control of every aspect of inmates' lives.

Inmates in maximum-security prisons are locked inside their cells following an early dinner in the mid-afternoon, and their doors are not opened again until the following morning.

Besides the double bunk, toilet and washbasin, actual living
space in a cell is non-existent. Shane provided an analogy
during one of our conversations: he told me that if I wanted
a realistic idea of what it's like to call a prison cell home
I should take a single mattress with me and move into my
bathroom for a weekend—then I should imagine having
to share the space with a complete stranger.

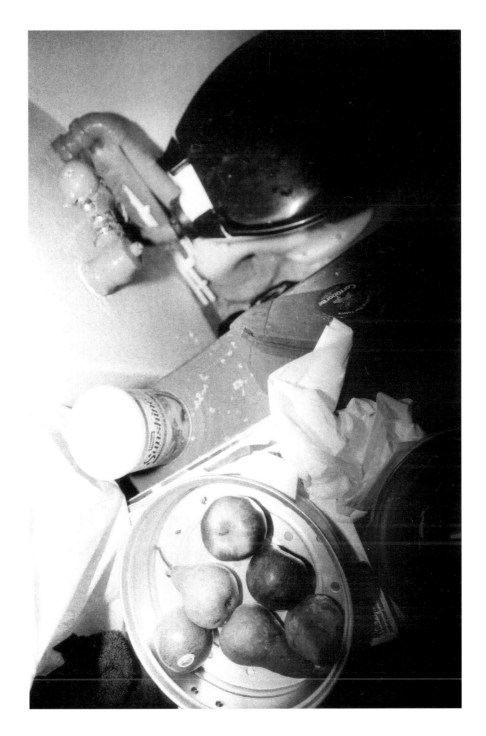

Jason: In jail there's someone always in your face, you've got no privacy. Like, you've got a toilet in your cell and when you have to go, you have to go.

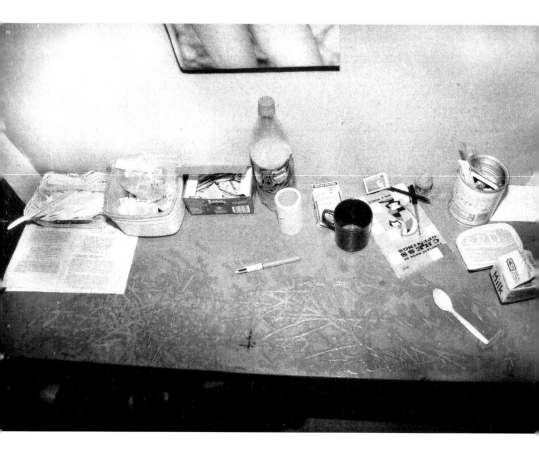

Within their small confines inmates go to great lengths to personalise their space ... they attempt to give the cold stark walls a sense of homeliness.

DARREN: I took advantage once. I asked for a pair of shoes with a bloke behind me. I said, 'Me mate's looking at ten years, you know, so he wants a pair of shoes, mate'. The bloke says no. I said, 'You sure?' He said 'Yep'. I said, 'Good man'. Because I didn't want to do it. I walked away and said, 'He ain't giving nothing' and after that we become all right friends. I apologised for it later. I haven't got the right to just go and take it, I know that and I ain't gonna put myself down or act like a gutter rat because I need something.

AUTHOR: How do you feel when you see it happening to others?

DARREN: I had a mate who got raped and I basically said, 'It happened, move on, get on with it, mate'. What else can you say? I don't want to say sorry because to me sorry means nothing. I feel sorry for them, of course, it shouldn't happen, no-one should get raped but he did, let's move on. But still I don't think any man or woman deserves to be raped.

I was with a young bloke who got raped in Cessnock by a bloke who'd just done sixteen or seventeen years. The governor put him in with this bloke. And this bloke said to him, 'I know where your mother lives, I'll get her if you don't bend over'. Well, the young fellow is only eighteen years old, just come to jail, didn't know nothing, so he done what he was told. The governor had no right putting him in with someone like that, who's just done seventeen years and was in for rape—that's a bit much.

He told what happened, so they sent the predator off on the sex program—like, is that going to help?

The young fellow, he went into protection, all because someone violated him. The governor, he come and seen us and said, 'Listen, can you look out for him if we send him back out from protection?' I said, 'No. I like the young man, I respect him, but he's obviously told you what happened—that cannot happen'. If he'd come out he would have been dead or stabbed or whatever, so his best response is to stay in protection. Very, very unfortunate but that's the way it goes, that's the way it's got to be.

Gordon counts his time in jail in decades and his time as a free, adult member of society in months. He has seen periods of violence in prison followed by a lull. Often what sparks the violence is a small matter; such is the nature of a constantly tense environment that is under the surveillance of officers, some of whom exacerbate the situation.

GORDON: I've always seen the violence as coming in waves. Like, there'll be that lull between the waves always. Screws are dogs, right? They've got to be the most putrid fucking people I've ever come across. I mean, look, there are some prison officers—they've got to be the worst I've ever come across. At anytime their attitude is 'give them nothing'. And when you're banged up in the yard all day and then you're banged up in the cell all night, after a period of time that becomes unsettling, right? And it becomes easy to react to situations.

Violence can erupt at any time, for no apparent reason.

MICHAEL: I've seen people get stabbed for stupid, idiotic things—over a box of matches, stabbed, like, thirty-something times, thirty-something holes in him and he still lived. Just over idiotic things.

AUTHOR: When do you become most violent?

MICHAEL: I'm violent when I'm on drugs. I was dependent on heroin from nineteen and I know what I'm capable of doing ... to get it and, yeah, I could be very violent. All I could see was that I needed that drug and if you're going to get in my way you're going to get belted. That was the mentality I had at the time. And [I was] also [violent] towards my de facto when I was young and stupid and jealous. I was a jealous person and that was very useless violence. I was young and immature. That's no justification for what I've done, I know that it was wrong.

AUTHOR: In prison, do some inmates beat others just for the hell of it?

MICHAEL: Yeah, I've seen that every day but I'm not like that. I'd been there before too, do you know what I mean? I'd experienced it to an extent. I've been picked on at home and I think maybe that I knew what they were feeling, so I didn't want to put that onto anyone.

AUTHOR: Then again, people who experience violence may want to inflict it on others in turn, because it's what they know.

MICHAEL: I did that too but not for a long period. I did that at school, like when I was telling you I was [cricket and soccer] captain—I'd [have] done that then if anyone barked in my ear.

AUTHOR: How do you deal with it when you see horrible things going on around you?

MICHAEL: Part of me switches off. You know it's got nothing to do with you, you know you can get into trouble if you stick your nose in it, you know a lot of possibilities that can happen. It's got nothing to do with me, so I don't stick my nose in.

And that was in boys' homes too to an extent, but it's a bit more extreme in jail. In boys' homes people aren't doing life; they're being released and they have got things to look forward to.

In jail, if it didn't concern me you just don't stick your nose in. A lot of people do it now but when I first got to jail, if it didn't concern you and you stuck your nose in you got dealt with, you know what I mean?

AUTHOR: Did you have to earn respect?

MICHAEL: I suppose most people probably said, 'Oh, this bloke, he'll have a go'. And that's the main thing that I've noticed throughout my whole time in jail, that predators in the system won't pick on people they know will stand up for themselves. But even if they know that you'll stand up and do your best it's not good enough, they'll still come after you, so you've got to make them aware of what you're capable of, they've got to hear what your reputation is … I had a few fights. I was a bit scared that I'd get belted and that happened on a few occasions. But other than that, no problems.

I put it to Michael that for inmates serving long sentences there is a time some years into their incarceration when there appears to be no light at the end of the tunnel. With no hope in sight, do they act as if they have nothing left to lose?

MICHAEL: There's a lot to lose but I don't think they see that. Like, I'm doing ten or over now and I know what I was capable of at the start of that lagging. But I've grown up a lot, I know I'm stronger now.

AUTHOR: How do you cope with it?

MICHAEL: You've just got to cop it on the chin, mate, and do your time. You get used to it and you learn to break it down with activities. You learn to play the system; you never beat the system unless you beat them at their own game. You don't learn that straight off the bat; that comes with knowledge, and knowledge is power.

There is rich subtext in prison that goes on well beyond the visibility of officers and staff. With so little control over their lives and so much time on their hands it is no surprise that inmates spend much of it creating rorts, scams and tricks. Our conversations in this area were limited by the fact that these inmates were currently serving sentences and were not in a position to publicise any illegal scams or reveal drug supply routes

Michael shared with me how one can avoid sharing a cell.

MICHAEL: Like, if you don't want to be two-out, you know how the game is played and you see a psych, have a yarn and spin them pure fucking shit just to

get this certificate for a one-on-one cell. That's the only way, 'cause if you were just to go and ask an officer, you can have one if they've got them available but as soon as they need to chuck someone in there because they're short for room you're getting a cell-mate. Whereas, if you have a medical certificate and it's backed up by your doctor as well it's hard for them, it's a lot of paperwork. That's how you beat them at their own rules; you can't beat them any other way. It's a system, there are rules and they've got to enforce the rules, it's their job, and the only way you can beat them is if you're not breaking the rules, you're just bending them ... and you're not going to get them in trouble, they've got their arse covered as well.

Prison is arguably the only public institution in which Indigenous Australians constitute the largest group; and in prison the advantage of numbers is primary.

DAVID: If I go in the shower and I've got three of the Koori boys there with me, if I know someone is behind me pulling out a knife I know the other three would be into it straightaway without hesitation. We're always watching each other. That's why we're so close; we call each other 'brother' and 'cousin' [and] we won't let [anything] happen to anybody. When we're in jail it brings us closer. I call a friend someone who would die for you, and all the Kooris are like that. I've never heard of another race stabbing a Koori, because that starts a war in another jail and everybody is going to pay for it. We ... look at it: they took our land off us, let's get them.

We get on pretty good, we don't like to fight in front of other races, we like to sort our own problems out when no-one else is around. When we fight in front of other races, that makes us weaker, that's when other races can get us, when we split up. So we keep it between ourselves, sort it out real quietly. The elders, they tell us what to do. There's no knives between ourselves, just little fights, just punch-ups and it's over with the next day.

When I asked the other inmates if they had become more, or less, racist while in prison they expressed fear of Indigenous inmates, who have a reputation for ruthlessness.

JASON: I tend to get on with everybody, but the ones that jail has made me dislike and stay away from is the Kooris because I found they're the ones who cause a lot of the problems. They stand over people for a lot of stuff, walk over to a bloke and say, 'Give us your shoes' and if he doesn't give it to them they'll bash him and take it. I've seen that a lot. But don't get me wrong, I've still got a couple of Koori friends. There's good and bad in every culture, some just have a lot more bad.

DARREN: The Kooris, they're just full of hatred. In Bathurst I'd say for every fifty Kooris you might have ten whites; it was horrible, what an atmosphere. To me they should make a jail for Kooris, a jail for Lebanese or wogs or whoever and leave the rest to us, because white people don't stand over white people, not really anyway. The blokes who do it are mainly Kooris, so why not isolate 'em? Let 'em stand over each other, stab each other—beautiful. In that prison, black rules, mate. Like, they don't just target anybody, they target the weak, the vulnerable.

Because I know a fair few of them I was basically all right. If I had any problems I'd go and see my Koori mates and they'd go and fix it.

Personally I think what we should have done when the different races come in—we being the superior being— we should have deadset put 'em in a tow and kept them there. Maybe stabbed a few, maybe killed a few to show we are the superiors. Unfortunately, we as a white community inside these walls are very divided. It's every man for themselves basically, where every nationality, they're all together; you want to fight one, you fight them all.

While he is Aboriginal himself, Michael was surprised to discover the fear of Aboriginal Australians when he first entered prison.

MICHAEL: I recall coming to jail and two Australians playing pool and I put a knock in to play next and they just played on without me and they didn't acknowledge that I was there, and I was like, 'Hey, what are you doing, I put a knock in'. I was only eighteen and I was locked in the wing, so I didn't have my family or friends, I only had a few of us that was in there and we were outnumbered. But because I stood my ground at the pool table and there was only those two playing, they put the pool balls and cue down and both left, so I had no-one to play against.

That was strange for me, that was the first time I ever came across that, and I was like, what's happening here? In my head I had thoughts, 'Fuck, they're going to get a knife or something'. I actually put pool balls in my pocket, just my defence mechanism sort of thing. But I waited, like, ten, fifteen minutes and they didn't come back. I was still wary so I didn't really muck around long and I cut down to a friend's cell and I sat down and just dwelled on it for another half an hour. And ... I'd seen my best mate the next day in the yard and I told him about it and that's when I started hearing that we didn't have nothing in jail before like this. It's only now that we stick up for ourselves in jail and do what had to be done. They know that we're here now and they know that we're not going to cop it on the chin anymore. But before that, blackfellas got nothing, got spat on.

David told me that the view among Indigenous inmates is that it is payback time—vulnerable white inmates receive punishment and retribution for the suffering of Indigenous Australians at the hands of white society. In prison, the tables are turned and inmates feel justified in using this strength to inflict torture on others and be entertained in the process. David discussed this subject openly, and I found it difficult to listen to him describe the useless violence he perpetrated. His victims, originally sentenced to a loss of liberty, were to endure much worse.

DAVID: When I talk to people I can see if they've got fear in them. And if [we] see that fear, look out, we'll just terrorise you. I'll stare at a lot of blokes. They put their head down and I know I've got this bloke. If they're staring at me I'll go up ... 'What are you staring at?', so I'll pull their bluff. They'll say, 'Nothing' and I say, 'You stare at me again I'll smash you, you cunt'. You'll stare at them all the time. It's just a fear game, it's all one big game, it's just the way you play it. If you don't show your fear, if you stand up for what you believe in, we'll respect you. We'll flog you but we'll still respect you afterwards. But if you don't we'll send you to the boneyard—protection. And once you go in there there's no turning back, you're a give-up and no good ... I've seen a lot of people die over that, just for telling on someone. It's not on. It's just the rules we've been brought up on.

As soon as we'd see a whitefella we'd give them the filthiest look. We used to make them sit on toilets in the yard all day and not get up from it ... when they're by themselves they're weak as piss but when they're around people they're different. It's just a daily routine. That's how it goes. That's how we get a lot of whitefellas back. And we do hurt 'em and that. We used to, like, make them cry, make them stick eggs in their arse in front of us so we laugh at them ... and we used to make a bloke rape 'em in front of us and laugh at 'em, and that's because that's what used to happen to our people. And we let them know: this is what happens, this is what your ancestors did to mine. It was like a payback.

At the time of our interviews, David was taking part in the VPP. Among the other inmates working through the VPP, he recognised some that he has tortured in the past.

DAVID: It's funny, you know, because most of [the] blokes in [the VPP] have got violent problems, and we used to make them cry and stuff like that, make them walk around the wing acting like a chicken or something or barking around the wing like a dog. Just terrorising them for a laugh. We used to do that every day because we liked to laugh … we'd pick on people so we can get a laugh, see how much we can hurt him until he gives in and stuff like that.

People on the outside might think it's nothing but to us a laugh a day is everything. Like, they stopped it now, having drag queens in the main—they're the ones you get your laugh from. When we used to be at Goulburn we used to play tackle football against different races. Used to be, like, ten to fifteen drag queens up there, they're named Sharon, Tracy, they're full-on, they are, the way they talk and that, it's just too much. When they knew it was a football match going on, they used to go up to Education and get the toilet paper and paint it, make streamers, stuff like that, do their hair up in ponytails, get the singlets and make miniskirts out of them and their shirts tied up. They'd be the cheer squad. They'd be fifteen of them. They'd make us laugh too much the way they'd go on. Used to get a laugh.

We used to love when there was drag queens in the wing and that, the young blokes, like, sucking them off and shit like that. They'll do anything, the more the merrier. Most of them now, they've got the Billy Ray, the virus, like the singer Billy Ray Cyrus—that's what we call it. Most of them have got AIDS now. That's how come they put all the draggies in protection now. We used to get them—the ones with the AIDS—to root this bloke, pass that on to him. We laugh about stuff like that—kill 'em slowly.

AUTHOR: Would you torment the same people each time?

DAVID: A couple of people. Once we torment someone we keep doing it. If he keeps quiet, keeps his mouth shut and doesn't tell no-one what's going on we'll respect him for that and we'll start laying off him a bit but we still let him know what's going on.

AUTHOR: Did you ever feel sorry for the person?

DAVID: It's revenge; like, my mum was taken away so I don't give a fuck about 'em. Even though it's not them but we just don't care. Maybe a little bit, especially since there was a march in Melbourne, too; they marched there ... didn't they?

Australia is a racist country, especially the redneck Howard and that. He needs to be killed. A lot of us talk about it in jail: knock him off and stuff like that. It's not going to change until he gets out; he's just a redneck. But I'm starting to realise it's not all Australians that feel like that. I've heard that, but it's really hard to believe ... there's always the majority and you can't trust it. It's been very hard for a lot of us. You can't trust the whitefella; we know how the government works, they just lie to you constantly.

They've got to realise this ... happened not long ago. What we do here in jail is nothing to what we copped all our lives. They don't know what racism is. I used to be so racist, deadset. I used to hate those sorts of whitefellas. We used to bash them till they turned black and blue.

AUTHOR: What about when people pleaded with you, cried out?

DAVID: We'd sell them. Make them root blokes. We'll sell their arse for a couple of packs of weed and that, let this bloke root you or something.

AUTHOR: Is it forced or is it consented?

DAVID: It's forced at the start when we tell them, but then it's consented.

AUTHOR: How does somebody come to terms with that?

DAVID: It's their life, mate, it's their fucking life. Is your life more important than sucking a dick?

AUTHOR: Do they become depressed and withdrawn?

DAVID: They feel bad and we laugh at them. 'You silly cow, why did you do that? What did you do that for?' We'll make fun of them. It's funny from our point of view. The way we look at it, how can a man do that to another man? I'd prefer to die than do that. Some of the other races will do that. We look at 'em and go, 'You're sad, you're fucking weak cunts. How can you let anybody put you down and tell you what to do?'

With a twist of logic, David regarded his victims of abuse as weak and pathetic for acquiescing to their perpetrators, yet recognised that to not do so would almost certainly mean death. The hypocrisy of such thinking never occurred to him; just as he rationalised attacking gay men as church sanctioned. It was useless violence and those victims who did not fight back, and even some that did, suffered abuse.

DAVID: I've done two-out with a couple of Aussie blokes and I tied 'em up to my toilet, tied them up to their bed. And when the screws opened up the door they're, like, gagged, tied up on the bed and I said, 'Get him out of here; the next time he'll be under the bed'. So they don't like putting other races with us Kooris.

Sometimes I understand it's wrong. But there is a lot of resistance in me to change, because I hate white people telling me what to do.

We're probably the more racist people in jail then anywhere, even the other races and that. We hate all kinds. This is how it works. But I've changed a bit, don't get me wrong.

You've got to use their system to your advantage or the system will use you to their advantage. I want to get out and say, 'I got the system, the system didn't do it to me, I beat the system', and that's what it's like for all of us.

AUTHOR: How do you feel about Indigenous officers?

DAVID: When I see Koori screws I just think, 'How could they?' There are probably more Aboriginal people locked up than any other race. I look at them: how could they do that? They're part of the English system [that] we're totally against. Some screws are deadset rednecks, so we treat them like rednecks; we'll spit on them, if we get a chance we'll flog 'em too. As soon as they walk into a wing and there's no other officer we'll jump him. Some of them they treat you like a person, so we'll treat them back like a person. All depends on how the officer is.

The way I used to look at it, these were the cunts

we used to pick on at school and that. These are the young blokes who we used to pick on, take their lunch money. They're just getting back at us, that's what we used to say. But they get really scared and that; we try and find out where they live and we tell 'em and they shit themselves. Hoping they'll go to another jail or you'll get kicked and you never see them again.

The inmates concurred that there were changes afoot in jail culture—in the types of officers and inmates going through the system—creating a more intense atmosphere with less solidarity among inmates. Overall, they see it as becoming a more violent place. They feel that our prisons are filling with young people who act like gangsters and that the old codes of behaviour among inmates, that offered some order, have given way to chaos and a greater sense of insecurity.

I asked Gordon, the longest-serving inmate, to offer his reflections on prison during both his earlier days of incarceration and today.

GORDON: When we had a fight it was one-on-one, no-one else jumped in. It was just one-on-one and when you finished you shook hands and walked away, and nine times out of ten you'd become good friends, close good friends.

AUTHOR: It's not like that now?

GORDON: Nah, now they're too quick to pull the blades out. These days, you know, the little motherfuckers want to fucking come and stab you.

Living in the Jungle

AUTHOR: What has happened?

GORDON: The system went too soft. You got some imbeciles, right? They're nothing outside, right? You know, they might have gone through boys' homes and got mollycoddled. When I went through boys' homes we had to march everywhere, we had work parties, but that was really good regimentation and we respected each other. Well, that's where it starts. When I went through boys' homes I'd only seen five or six [people] I went through with end up in jail.

They go through now and they get everything fucking handed to them on a silver platter and that's fucking spoiling them. And that's why I said when they get to prison they've got nothing and they know that they can just go and take what they fucking want. Hence, drama.

We were talking about this yesterday in our group, you know; like, you'd get into fucking fights with these little cunts that are in here now; like, the little gangs of kids that get around now. The scary part for me is that I'll kill one of the little things and spend the rest of my life in here. That's the scary part. They don't scare me. I know this sounds like bravado and that, but that's how I've been all my life.

SHANE: It used to be that you used to go to a jail and people would go, 'Oh, you need this or that? What do you need?', and now people are more self-centred, more selfish. You've got your gangster sort of type in here, and you have the misfits, then you've got the white-collar crims who stick together, and the Asians, Kooris and Lebs also all stick together. You've got your little groups all around.

Prison violence is also related to race and tensions between ethnically-related crime gangs. Increasing violence between racial groups led to a policy of segregation in some prisons, where each ethnic groups shares its own wing. This is not the case in Long Bay, where inmates from different ethnic backgrounds are mixed together.

DAVID: The Chinese and Kooris, we stick together, we're one gang. We used to be together years ago, all Islanders and Kooris—this is in the '80s and early '90s. Then the drug scene come in with the Vietnamese, and the Vietnamese and the Islanders got together. It starts from the outside and finishes off inside, because all them shootings, they get finished off in here, all the shoot-outs. If somebody gets shot outside we'll fix it up in here.

That's how the big wars with the Lebanese and Kooris started. It started in Goulburn '97 and '98 over something stupid: a Turkish fella who grew up with a lot of the Redfern boys—a lot of my mates—he done the wrong thing to this Lebanese. And the Lebanese— about six of them—tried to stab him and they were chasing him all round the yard when all the Kooris seen it, jumped in and stopped it, because [the Lebanese] were going to kill him. And it was a big war up [at] Lithgow. So the Chinese and Kooris joined forces and the Lebanese, Vietnamese and Islanders all joined forces against us.

MICHAEL: They should have left jail the way it was run and they knew this. It's causing more dramas, causing more conflicts, and that's something that I've seen with my own eyes … I've been in a jail when it wasn't like that and we used to all congregate together and there was hardly any conflict. Sure, there was a conflict here and there and a drama here and there, but not on the scale that it's on today, you know what I mean?

If you're a whitefella and I'm a blackfella and we had a disagreement but you've got twenty Aussies behind you and I've got twenty black Aboriginals behind me, we're going to have a fight, one-one-one, me and you, that's it. If one of your mates jumps in then one of my mates can jump in, like if one of my mates jumps in well then one of your mates can jump in. And that doesn't happen; if we just fight one-on-one that's how it is.

If you pull a knife out then I pull a knife out, you know what I mean? It's just whether you're capable of using that knife and if you're willing enough to go the whole hog, I suppose. But if they didn't separate us into separate yards then a lot of it wouldn't happen; it wouldn't have started in the first place, so it wouldn't have eventuated to where it is now.

One outcome of housing inmates separately is that as they are moved around various prisons during their term, conflict between individual inmates can escalate and become an issue between the different ethnic groups as friends get involved.

MICHAEL: A lot of it is over drugs, and when their race is locked in a separate yard then that person can't be gotten. And that person says a lot of things that shouldn't be said and a lot of lies and it causes a lot of chaos. And word could be spread, inmates move from that jail to this jail, and then this jail knows about it so they attack that race there.

It's like dog eat dog. Like, whoever forms the strongest group is going to dominate, so you can't be on your own. I've got to get a group and maybe I'll survive; I'm not going to survive on my own. That's the mentality, whereas it never used to be like that.

Today, jail is all about reputations, it's not about solidarity. It's just not the jail I was brought up in, it's not jail that I want to be a part of, you know what I mean?

While inmates still hate prison officers—and the penalty for consorting with them can be high, even deadly in maximum-security—there is a gradual improvement in relations. Some of the inmates believed this has been achieved by creating more rifts among inmates.

MICHAEL: When I first came to jail we respected each other in green—respect because you were in green and they're in blue. They're our enemy not you, mate, you know what I mean? You committed a crime and you came into jail and you're doing your time and that's enough for me to respect you. To me, that's what jail should be because that's something that I was brought up on and shown early on in jail, and I saw a lot of good things from that. Whether he was a spinner and hearing things or on medication and tripping out, it didn't matter, whereas today if you are like that you get picked on and you get belted for no reason at all. Today it's not us against them, it's just the racial gang warfare, like Asians or Aboriginals and Islanders and Lebs, and in the middle of it [are] Aussies.

It was us against them, it was blue against greens, and now it's us against us. They've taken themselves out of the equation and they've made their job a lot easier for themselves. They knew what they were doing by separating us in yards in Goulburn jail, Maitland jail.

JASON: Back then it used to be the green against the blue but now it's the green against the green and the green against the blue. There's a lot of green people wearing blue—inmates that act like screws. There's no real solidarity to the inmates anymore; I think because of drugs some people lose their morals.

The changes in relations between inmates and officers may also be due to a progressive recruitment policy, over the past two decades since the Nagle Royal Commission into prison violence, of hiring more empathic officers with greater life experience. None of the inmates had stories of systematic abuse by officers of an inmate. Instead they described a range of individuals from understanding to sadistic.

SHANE: Years ago they wanted tough, hard bastards who wouldn't cop shit and would just bash people. Now they're trying to get better educated people that are more down to earth, understanding; people who can communicate well.

They implemented case management some time back, to break down the barrier between the green and the blue. You've got a case manager who sits down asking if I've got any problems and taking notes. I sort of agree with it if it can break down any dramas. If they can break that down in any way, well and good, but I believe it's really just another way of gathering intelligence about us. In the whole time case management has been going on, maybe seven years, I've probably needed my case manager about once or twice, to just chase things up. I don't tell them any of my personal business because I don't think they need to know about that. I don't divulge any personal information to anybody that I don't trust and anyone I don't know.

DARREN: You get good and bad officers; the majority to me are arrogant and what not. That's only because I'm a crim. If I was someone like yourself, I'd see them all the same, basically. But you sit long enough with them and you'd be getting to see who's bad and what not, who's two-faced and stuff like that. On this program you have to talk to them; there's no way out of it. In other jails you'd just go, 'Yeah, piss off, you dog' and just walk away. Here you have to tolerate them; if you don't you're out of the program. That's what they have over you. I've got officers who are nineteen or twenty telling me what to do. I'm twenty-seven years old, mate. They've been here three to six months, I've been here for eight years—who the hell are they?

Most of the inmates I spoke with were taking part in the VPP. Through extensive individual and group counselling they are taught to re-examine their reactions to events and hopefully break the cycle of violence they are accustomed to. The VPP encourages interaction between inmates and officers, a sharp contrast to relations elsewhere in prison.

DARREN: Since I've been here it's been relaxing. I was saying to an officer this morning, I said, 'If we were in another jail I'd be calling you stuff, but because I'm here I have to talk to you. If I don't we get done for "no communication", we get kicked out'. I said, 'And then when I leave here people bag [me] because [I] talk to you ... so how the hell do [I] win?' So you have to watch what you say. I said to her, 'When I'm not with people I'll talk to you all day, mate, but when I'm with friends or people see me, then it's a bit hard'. You get stabbed; it's that easy.

Darren did not take well to learning that his cousin was a correctional officer, a fact he only discovered when he came across him unexpectedly in prison.

DARREN: My own cousin, mate, I threatened to deadset bash him because he's an officer. To me, no family member should be locking up another human being. Next couple of days he was gone. I knew he was my cousin but I [had not] seen him for thirteen years. He said, 'How are you going?' and I said, 'Who the hell are you, mate? Don't speak to me'. He said, 'Don't you recognise me?' I said, 'Why would I, you're a dog ... What are you doing, mate? Where is your morals? Listen, speak to me again and I'll chop into you.' I never told anybody—could have got me killed; it still might because people don't let go of stuff like that. To me it would be justified even though I'd done nothing wrong—it's just a code that we've got.

Rehabilitation requires the learning and expression of appropriate emotions. Yet in prison society there is no place for these. In fact, prison demands quite the opposite: the suppression of emotions. Housing criminals in such an environment is punitive but not rehabilitative, something the inmates in the VPP have come to realise.

AUTHOR: You were saying to me that you do your own time, you've got to be tough. So you're thinking like that, then you get a visit from your wife and emotions start running ...

GORDON: Yeah, tell me about it.

AUTHOR: ... and then you've got to go back to your cell.

GORDON: And walking back to your cell ... like in Lithgow, I'd fucking walk back under a covered pathway and there'd be fucking cunts there and I'm in dream world, I'm with my wife, right? I'm still talking to her and, you know, my radar should be fucking working but it's not there, it's impaired. As soon as I get challenged—boom, back to reality.

I asked David and Darren whether they ever allowed themselves to feel vulnerable—to cry, for example.

AUTHOR: Have there been moments when you've cried, alone in your cell?

DAVID: I haven't cried for years, mate. Last time I cried was when me girlfriend passed away. That crushed me, that did. I don't even bother to think about it because then I start doing it hard. I hold a lot in. You can't show your emotions in jail. The strong would take advantage of you. When I'm having a really bad day I take it out on other people. That's when I fight ... that's when I hurt other people. It's the only time I hurt other people, when I got problems on the outside. I throw it on someone else, get all me pain out on them. That's how I deal with it.

DARREN: You've got to hold back, you've got to know what to say and when to say it. Like, I cry in here, don't worry about that, but you don't do it in front of people, you basically do it alone. I only cry when I'm talking about my mother, that's all I've got basically, so that's very emotional. But I suppose if I got stabbed or kicked in the guts and [someone] jumped all over my head, I suppose I'd have a couple of tears. But it's not a place for whining, that's a sign of weakness. I've got friends who say, 'Des, do what you want to, if you want to cry have a cry, mate'. Yeah, but people see this and you're gone. I don't think everyone is as hard as what they say but it's the way that they've got to come across.

Chapter 6:
The Revolving Door

In theory, prison is the kind of experience that, once had, will never be had again. The reality is, however, that prison is a revolving door for too many inmates.

At the moment over 50 per cent of currently serving inmates in New South Wales have served time before.[34] It is clear they have not been rehabilitated—they were released with the same underlying issues that led them to commit crime in the first place, only now they are angrier and even more socially inept.

One prison officer recounted to me a story of an inmate who was released during the officer's Friday shift and was back in custody by his Monday shift. 'To some of them I no longer say goodbye,' he lamented, 'just "see you later"'.

Consider what happens to inmates once their sentence has been completed and the prison gates are unlocked. Inmates without family or friends to greet them find themselves standing at the bus stop with their few possessions, a little money and a desire to never come back. After living in the confines of prison society, however, the world can seem an overwhelming place. In prison they knew how things worked, and the longer they were in for the better they were acclimatised (or institutionalised). Outside, they are lost. Yearning for familiarity, most return to their old neighbourhoods and friends—if any have remained in contact with them—or to the temporary accommodation of a friend's lounge, possibly someone they met in jail.

With no assets, few skills and a résumé guaranteed to ward off employers and landlords, former inmates find their levels of frustration and stress rise, and commonly satiate this with alcohol and drug use—the latter being a habit that they may have formed while incarcerated.

Upon release it is also common for inmates to experience the stigma of imprisonment; some feel that others can somehow tell they are former inmates simply by looking at them, and consequently view them with condescension.

Many released inmates are angry at the system that denied their freedom and are, in effect, still at war with society. And it is society that bears the brunt of this anger.

> JASON: I had one mate who has been in and out; I've seen him three times in the last four years. And every time I see him it's, 'I'm sick of this, I just want to get out, I've had enough', and I tell him, 'Do something about it, learn some skills, something that is going to help you stay out'. He's probably been put down that much in his life and he's put himself [down] that much he needs something dramatic to happen to him before he'll change.

Shane's prison record is an example of prison's revolving door syndrome. Once each sentence was served he would return to his old friends and haunts and become immersed in their lifestyle. Even when he decided to change his ways for the better, his emotional problems would overwhelm him and he would revert back.

> SHANE: When I had twelve months to go on the sentence, I was placed in a pre-works release program. The

first job I got was building truck trailers, and in the first month that I'd been there I built, on my own, a truck trailer. I was overawed—I'd just built a five-tonne trailer. The satisfaction was unbelievable. But I ended up stuffing up, just a spur of the moment thing. I had a smoke of pot one day and I did the dirty urine and I ended up going back to maximum-security with eight months to go.

But when I got out I wrote to the same company explaining everything and was surprised that they offered me a job. I worked for them for probably another year and then I did something again and was sent back to jail with another twelve-month sentence. I was knocking around with other guys from jail; none of them were working and I just went along for the ride. I didn't need the money since I was doing pretty well, but I was using a few drugs here and there and then one thing leads to another and you go out and commit a crime.

I went to Long Bay, and that sentence was over before I knew it. But I walked out of jail with nothing, and there's nothing worse then being thrown out the gate and not having anywhere to go and not having any employment lined up. You're just thrown out in the big wide world thinking, 'Where am I going tonight? Where am I eating tomorrow?' You're behind the eight ball from the word go. I couldn't do it. I tried to get some-where to live and [was] knocked back because I'd been in jail. I had only been out of jail three months and I did a robbery with another bloke. So I'm back inside.

But while he was out, Shane met a woman, and the relationship continued while Shane was incarcerated, creating pressures he was unable to handle.

SHANE: It was love at first sight between us, and two weeks after I got to know her I'm pinched again and in jail. And I really liked this girl and didn't want to lose her. When I was taken into custody I rang her, explained the situation and told her I was really sorry. The next morning I walked into court and there she was, prepared to put up bail. It was the first time in [my] life that anybody had come to court for me; even my family had never been to court prior to this, and here's this lady I was just starting to know. Down in the cell I had a bit of a cry about it.

She said, 'I don't care what you've done, I don't want to lose you'. It was the first time anything good like that happened to me in a long, long time. When I did end up going to get sentenced the judge agreed that the best opportunity for me was with this woman. She actually got my father to come to court that day to make it try and look as good as possible. I couldn't have asked for more than that. I had already served a few months, so I now only had a year or so to go.

I was getting day leave and everything is going well, we were getting on top of things, I was saving money. But I learnt that behind the scenes I've got prison officers trying to proposition her. They're all trying to basically get in her pants. When I found out about it I lost the plot. I felt helpless and fucking betrayed by these arseholes.

Shane was the only inmate I spoke with who had escaped from prison. This act earned him an 'E' classification, signifying escapee, ensuring his remaining days in prison are spent in maximum-security facilities.

SHANE: One day I came back from day leave and had to give a urine test; I had four months left in jail at this stage. One of the officers who was giving her a hard time tried [to get] me to do a urine test in a jar with another guy's name on it. They had a box of brand new jars and I said, 'Give me one of those and I'll piss in it'. So I'm charged for not complying and taken off day leave and works release, all because this piece of shit wants to get into my de facto. I went to welfare and to see the deputy governor, tried to explain things, and they were basically saying this didn't happen and they didn't want anything to do with it. I was being harassed and I was in a position where I couldn't do anything. I was in a corner. So I escaped.

It was alleged that I drove out of the complex dressed as a prison officer in a prison motor vehicle. I wanted to find out what's really been going on. She kept a lot secret from me because she didn't want me to go ballistic in jail, do something I might have regretted.

I was caught, and fronted a lady magistrate, explained the whole situation to her, and she was just outraged. She understood why I had done what I had done and gave me a month. I nearly dropped dead—I was looking at two years. My girlfriend was in tears. Then I had to write to the parole board; [I] explained everything that had happened and they [gave] me my parole and I got out.

Newly released and living with the woman he loved, Shane's life was looking up. The emotional upheavals that followed, however, were too much for Shane to bear and he once again reverted to drugs.

SHANE: I learnt [that] a lot of other things were going on behind the scenes. I knew this woman was married but had been separated from this guy for twelve years. But they were still married and he couldn't come to terms with the fact that he'll never be with this woman again. He was always there because they had a son as well. He caused us so many problems. I was fighting with him and he was getting drunk and coming around. In the end I couldn't take it any more and said, 'It's either me or him' and shot through.

So I went back to the streets and started using drugs, running amuck and having to commit crimes and [was sent] back in jail. I got released on parole again and tried to reconcile with her, but things got worse and he was even more filthy on me. Three months later I'm pinched on sixty armed robbery charges. That's why I'm here now.

I was pleased about getting an eight-year sentence in some ways, because armed robbery carries a twenty-five year maximum. And I'd already done three of the eight, so that leaves five to go. But then I'm thinking, 'Fuck, I've got five years to go'; it's the longest sentence I'd ever done. Eight years is a long chunk of your life.

Darren too is caught in the revolving door—not only did he anticipate returning to prison after being released, but since I last spoke to him, he already had.

DARREN: After I got out of prison the first time I was supposed to go into rehab but I didn't turn up. I was just running around. I jumped on people's heads; I didn't care who it was, mainly foreigners, mainly wogs and that. I'd get back on the gear and that would be it. They put me away and now it was my turn to hurt society. I was most certainly angry, I would have liked to have hurt them all. But it wasn't the whole of society that put me in, it was me. I've only just come to realise that.

I used to go look for victims. Any woman, [but] not old women, I don't believe in hurting old women, like forty and up, I don't believe in it. I don't hurt 'em, I just take their money. That's it; like, it's no big deal. They're still victims of crime but they could end up with a lot more scars then just a couple of hundred dollars' worth, you know what I mean? They've also got to realise they were very lucky. If I was higher strung a little bit more it could have been a hell of a lot worse. Thank God it wasn't.

Getting caught was inevitable. No-one can stay on the run forever. It was getting more demanding and I had to 'do' more people. My second sentence was four months, then I got maybe six months and after that three months; they were, like, parole violations. Then when I got out I died from an OD; I had a cap and died. From there I went into hospital and got fixed up. I went back home, stayed in Mum's house for three or four days, maybe longer, until I was ready, and from there I went back to crime. That was my intention the whole lagging: to get out and use and see what I could do. I got out and I lasted fourteen months. In that time I'd do nine, ten bags a day.

The intention is to get what I can with the least amount of what I call punishment. I just want to grab the bag and see you later. If you want to play, we'll play, most certainly. If I have to I'll do what I have to, with no emotion whatsoever. If I didn't, I'm going to get pinched. The most dangerous person is some-

one who is hanging out [for a drug fix], because we don't care.

It got to the stage where I was that sick I just had to come to jail to get better. I was that sick of heroin I couldn't think unless I had gear in me, I couldn't function. I'd do $400 a day. I used to get $3500 or $4000 out of one day and I'd just go away to a motel for three or four days. When I got low [I'd] just go out again. So it was a constant routine; it's just like going to work, that was. I didn't like it but you have to do it. Unfortunately that's the way it went.

During one bag-snatching, Darren's victim resisted and he attempted to stab her in the throat, causing injury.

I got five years because I stabbed a woman in the throat when I was eighteen or nineteen. The woman wouldn't give me $1.20, so I thought, 'If you're not going to give it to me, I'm going to hurt you for it'. And unfortunately I had to do what I did to that poor lady, which was deadset stupid.

A prison officer pointed out to me that, for inmates, prison is a period of stagnation. An eighteen-year-old sentenced to spend the best part of a decade in prison emerges at the end of their prison term with the mindset of an eighteen-year-old. They have not had any of the normal experiences of life during those years. As noted earlier, inmates do not mature in prison. They leave with a mindset as immature as the one they entered prison with. Hence, adjusting to life on the outside is no simple matter and can lead to failure.

SHANE: I don't believe the answer is to build more jails and lock more people up. I think they should get to the nucleus of the problem. Instead of building a five hundred-bed jail build a five hundred-bed rehab program. Locking somebody up and sending them to jail for twelve months for a drug-related crime does not stop that person from using drugs or doing crime. They get thrown back out in the street twelve months later, they've got no family, they're depressed, they've got no money [and] obviously they're using drugs again straightaway to cope with the depression.

It's too late once they hit the jail system. They get caught up in this culture of being in institutions. They're not better off when they get out. Rehabilitation is not mandatory, it's not something that just happens when you come to jail.

Some countries offer an alternative to punitive forms of incarceration. In Scandinavia and the Netherlands, for example, inmates who are deemed suitable are housed in self-contained, individual cells that are operated as democratically run units with an almost 100 per cent staff-to-inmate ratio.[35] Normal social interaction and activities are encouraged, violence is rare and prison rape virtually unheard of.

Rather than attempting to punish these inmates beyond deprivation of their liberty, these systems aim to create a safer society by rehabilitating crime-prone individuals.

SHANE: I don't agree with the outside mentality of lock us up and throw away the key. What people aren't thinking is: what about when we are released? They want to lock us up and treat us like animals, but when we get out we'll still act like animals, and a lot of people don't realise that, don't understand that. It's not the answer. A lot of people who are doing crimes have got problems and they need to deal with their problems, they need to learn the skills to deal with their problems.

JASON: It's still that attitude on the outside that we should be locked up and throw away the key. By doing that and by giving us nothing and by throwing us in the yard and treating us like animals, they don't realise that we get let back into society and a lot of people get bitter because the system has messed them around, and they take it out on society. And jail breeds crime, it breeds violence, it breeds anger.

Not every inmate can be rehabilitated. Only those who are able and ready to recognise that the problem lies in their patterns of behaviour, and who wish to rectify these patterns, are candidates for change. This requires inmates to understand their emotional states, triggers and responses and particularly their aggression. Paradoxically, the prison code undermines any efforts at personal exploration, as within prison, expressions of emotions signify weakness. But, as the inmates tell me, behind the required facade of fearless invincibility, they hide a myriad of emotional issues that seldom, if ever, see the light of day. They are unable to express or make sense of their vulnerabilities.

JASON: Some people hide behind the drugs; some people put the big front on, big gangster sort of thing. Some people hide themselves away in the corner and you never see them. Then other people are social butterflies.

Definitely different ways they handle it. Some people get the positive out of it, but the majority probably dwell on the negative. There are a lot of people in jail who just will not take responsibility for their own actions. They have the 'poor me' syndrome. They blame everyone, but the last person they blame is themselves.

Despite his intentions to the contrary and his recent experiences in the VPP, Darren seems destined to experience the revolving door and treat prison as a surrogate home. He is yet to relinquish the erratic lifestyle of drugs and crime.

DARREN: I want to become a nine-to-five man, I want to be a citizen of a decent society; I don't want to be known as a criminal even though I'm always going to be labelled one. Love to have kids. I love children altogether. Would be nice to sit at home and play goo-gaas and blow on their guts and throw balls around. I had it done to me, so I'd like to do it to my kid [but] I've always said I don't want it while I'm in this predicament that I'm in.

I'm doing a hospitality course at the moment. I thought because I love being in the kitchen ... it could teach me something. It's all about the diseases in the kitchen, the cleanliness, the serving-up quantity and quality. It just gives me something to fall back on outside. I'd like to be a kitchen hand, to be quite honest. I want to work in hostels, cook for homeless people and stuff like that because I've been on the street, I've been there and done it, so I'd like to give a little back for what they gave me.

I get out in five months. I can't see it yet. I just wait till they call me to the reception room. Then I know it's over. If it's the first time you get out you look forward to it, you can't sleep, you get the knotty stomach and start talking all this mumbo jumbo about what you're going to do and who you're going to see, how many women, and all that crap. I'm just looking forward to going home and having a deadset decent meal.

AUTHOR: What about women?

DARREN: Never have been interested in girls. I was too busy drinking and drugging and thieving to worry about anything really. They say, 'Des, where's your woman?' and I say, 'I haven't had one for eight years, mate'. They say, 'Why not?' and I say, 'Why? I'm too busy using, I've got no time. Where am I going to take her, down to Cabramatta?' I said, 'When I wake up to myself and finish all the using, then I'll get a woman and start doing restaurants and the movies'. When you're a drug addict you can't do that.

AUTHOR: How will it be when you get out this time?

DARREN: I'm getting more mature now; I've got to get out of this rut. I've been in it far too long. The party is over. I would like to be a normal citizen. I'd like to have my own place, my own house and come home to the old welcome mat out the front, have dinner prepared, decent job, woman. My intention is not to go out and steal, I have no intention of it, as yet. The urge is maybe five months away but the urge isn't there.

AUTHOR: Where will you go when they open the gates?

DARREN: I don't want my mum to pick me up; I'll find my way home. Might take a day or two but I'll get home. I'll plod along, go here and go there. I might go into town for a day or so. Automatically I think I'll be searching as well, like, not meaning to but I'll be doing it. It's not as if I'm intending to do something but I will be looking, most certainly. There's a chance I'll do something, most certainly. If I get down and out or bored, why not?

My ideal of doing things is robbing people and I can't see anything beyond that or around it. I don't want to dress up and go to a restaurant or meet people and go … to … clubs. I don't want to do that shit. I need adrenaline. I don't do it by jumping off a bridge or going down a cliff or something, but inflicting, not so much pain but inflicting fear into people. That's what I like to do and that's it. For me it's not a feeling, it's just a necessity, [I've] just got to do it. I don't feel anything; if it's bad, if it's something hectic or I've stabbed somebody or something, later on down the track I'll think about it. I don't care about people.

AUTHOR: Do you think you'll come back to prison?

DARREN: I don't say I'll never come back here, because that just sets me up for a fall. There's a sixty–forty chance that I will be back. Hopefully not for a long time … I don't want to come [back] within the next six months or something.

There's nothing to be worried about here; you get everything. All you got to do is basically get up and go to work. You don't even have to do that. So what's the big deal? The only thing you lose is basically freedom and I personally don't even mind losing that. I could do *it for the rest of me life, to be quite honest with you. I just switch off. I honestly don't mind being locked in jail, I honestly don't.*

The inmates participating in the VPP were working to break the cycle of violence they lived inside and outside prison. But changing lifelong patterns of thinking and emotional responses in a matter of weeks is a big task, particularly when inmates are then returned to a mainstream prison where they have no use for their new skills and must once more suppress their emotions and vulnerabilities. For Stuart the VPP was the right program at the right time to learn about his violent tendencies.

STUART: I've learnt to control them now. I don't know what it is. I had a lot of pain, but hidden pain. I used to hide it. Pain that I couldn't solve, things I couldn't solve.

AUTHOR: What made you decide to do this program?

STUART: I voluntarily came here. I'd seen a psych back in the remand centre and I said I want to do the program to benefit me in the long run. Because what I did was wrong and I wanted to get some help in preparing myself ... to go out in society and ... not relapse.

By this time I had more self-esteem; I done a bit of jail now and I didn't have them worries that go through your head: Is this happening on the outside? Is this happening on the inside? The bad thoughts that you used to have in the early part of your sentence were all gone. You're thinking about what you could be doing today on the outside, and then all of a sudden it all comes back to that: understanding that you done that crime. And you try just to work out the crime and you try to work out where [you] could have fixed it. What could I have done? And it starts to work against you. You start to feel guilty.

Eventually you get burnt out and it just goes away. You just forget about it, you just put it in the cupboard and label it. It gets a lot easier. You feel more confident as you do time, you know, you're getting closer to the end. And you start to realise that you want to go home. The punishment is still there and it affects you every day. Something's said to you or you can't have something—it's punishment and you relate it back to why you're here.

And so I came into the program and I was all full of enthusiasm because I wanted to be here. The first stage of the program was pretty basic. And then you realise when you start to do the second stage of the program why ... the first stage is there; you must get trust with other inmates because you will be disclosing stuff to repair yourself. And if you don't learn how to do that in the first stage, you cannot do stage two, there's no way you can do it. Because if you dislike somebody and you don't want to say nothing to anybody or dislike officers ... you're not going to get the output. So, of the eight ... or ... nine blokes that I first come into the program with there's only me and another bloke left at the end of stage two.

They all got in trouble and moved on or were released. They don't want to change their old ways. All they want to do is come here for a free ride, but there's no benefit in that. It's here you stop it from coming back. I'm not going to say it's going to happen overnight, because blokes will come here and have got nearly twenty-five years of these bad thoughts going through their head, and there's criminal pride, and so it's very hard to fix it overnight. But if a situation comes up, it might be one thing out of the whole program that could stop you from committing a crime or could stop you from doing a bad thing and sending you back ... in here. Then the program's worked.

AUTHOR: Did you discover things about yourself through the program?

STUART: Yes, I did. One part of the program was [about] stress management ... there [are] a lot of problems in the world that happen that you can't deal with and that [causes] stress. Well, they give us this relaxation course, and we decided that we thought it was all a joke, 'go and lie down on the floor and stare up at the ceiling', 'close your eyes and think'. But after you do it a couple [of] times you start to realise the benefit. And then you're able to do it yourself, lie down and relax and not let anything get within you and destroy your thoughts. This has given me some ... benefits that I've never had before. I mean, you don't get these benefits at school, parents don't give you these benefits. What we do is we blame other people to not look at ourselves. That program made us look at the choices that we made.

AUTHOR: What did you discover about your anger?

STUART: I think a lot of our pain is anger ... we're angry with ourselves and we're angry with others because we look at other humans as inferior or they've got something we want, or something like that.

Prison culture is such that when inmates bump into each other accidentally, aggression can ensue; failure to respond in such situations can be considered a sign of weakness and encourage others to do it intentionally. I asked some of the inmates to consider how they would respond if someone in the outside world were to bump into them or invade their space.

> *STUART: [If] they bump us on the street, [what's] the first thing we do? We go in defensive because we believe we're in the right. We're not considering that maybe it's been an accident.*
>
> *And that is what they teach you here. If someone jumps in the line in front of you at the railway station, what do you do? Well, the first thing you're going to do if you have a criminal past and you're tough and strong, you're going to drag the bloke out.*
>
> *I probably would have done it. Okay, you know that if you go on and drag him out in front of a train, you're going in jail, all right? You know if you punch him, you're going to jail. You know if you even talk to him and ask him a question, you're putting yourself into a position where you could get into a conflict. If you ignore it, what do you say to yourself? What are the things you should say to yourself to save your-self? Well, 'Maybe he's running late or ...', but how far are you going to allow it to go? Are you going to allow another ten people to jump in front of you? Where does it stop? They [the VPP] give you ideas of how to deal with situations like that. Not every*

situation you're going to be able to deal with perfectly but it gives you some more options. And through ... the program so far, everything has been constructive and informal and it's given me new problem-solving skills.

AUTHOR: Are you still a violent person?

STUART: I could be. I used to have raged thoughts and if I acted on them ... there's no amount of things I could [not] have done. No-one could stop me. Now that's what I don't want. I hated that. I wanted to get to the basis of why that rage was there. I had an act of rage, okay, and a guy dies, okay? Now I have to look at myself for my own benefit because I don't want to do it again. This is why I came to the program, to give me some sort of feedback so that I can deal with society again and be put into a situation where I'm cornered and be able to deal with it in a way where it doesn't cause problems. And that whole build-up to that point of my crime was all my life just dealing with it in short spurts and not having a real good look at myself. So it's amazing you have to come to jail to find something.

I looked upon using the incarceration period as a learning point for me, because I don't want to make a mistake in life again. I mean, I will make mistakes, but I don't want to make a big giant one like that, where it just takes you away from society and puts you in this environment.

AUTHOR: How do you feel about prison now?

STUART: I don't like being incarcerated but it's given me time out from society, where I can go back over and look at mistakes and find out where I went wrong. Why do I go wrong? What do I want out of life? And it's amazing that I've found a place that I've adapted to. I'm building confidence to go back into society.

I'm building myself; I've got to start from scratch again. It's very hard to do. At one stage there I was going to give up. I was going to say: well, I'm useless to society. But I'm gaining composure. Why should I be alive? What can I contribute to my life? And what can I contribute to make me feel better? Because I do not feel good about myself for what has happened. And I'm starting to get that self-esteem again. I'm not saying that I wanted to but coming to jail has turned my life around.

AUTHOR: You seem to have recognised that there's no point in fighting the system. That's quite a different attitude to a lot of other inmates.

STUART: That's true. The system's beaten you already. You're being punished; you cannot fight the punishment. All they're doing is punishing themselves more, but they can't see that point.

After living in a society marked by perpetual stress and violence, the inmates found it difficult to learn to trust people and accept them without suspicion. Inmates must also learn to trust social institutions and understand that uniforms can represent public service rather than intimidation and aggression.

AUTHOR: Can you make friends in prison? Can you end up trusting people?

GORDON: Nah, I can't. I live with these blokes twenty-four hours a day and I only trust them up to a point, and nine times out of ten they will fucking go over that point—end of the friendship.

AUTHOR: It must be hard to learn to start to trust people again. I imagine that's part of what you're learning now?

GORDON: Yeah, more trust in the system for me. To not fight it, not rebel against it. That's why I rebelled against it all the time, disobeying the screws, toying with shit that I'm not supposed to do, you know, just rebelling against the system. Outside I was doing armed robberies, you know, you can't get more rebellious than that.

The VPP requires inmates to examine their inner demons, and to articulate them in front of others. This is no easy task and, as Darren experienced, can be quite painful.

DARREN: This program has made me more honest, more assertive. I've got more confidence in myself now. I could look in the mirror and say, 'I love you' ... I can look and say, 'Geez, you're good-looking, mate', and I'm proud of that. I'm clean-shaven, I don't walk around like a rebel or living in gutters. I feel like I can basically accomplish anything I put my mind to. But I have to get the deep and dark secrets out. I've got to let the demons out—like selling my body and stuff like that, trying to stab my mother, seeing her drunk, and everything like that. That might not sound bad to you but because I've had them for so long [there's] just shit that I have to release.

Selling myself I'd done the once and once only. At that time I had burnt all my bridges with every connection I had with family, aunties, the lot, and I had nowhere to turn and I was hungry. I regret it to this day and I always will. But there's nothing I can do about it; I don't hate myself for doing it because I done what I thought was right. But it's not for me, not for someone of the upbringing and the love that I had. Someone like that shouldn't do that. But I've experienced it and what can I say?

When I spoke about that incident here the other inmates gave me a hard time, they assumed I was a prostitute. Where they hell are they coming from? I couldn't understand it. They aren't open like I am. I don't talk to them anymore, disowned the lot of them. They can't understand why and I'm not going to tell them because they should be able to recognise or feel what I felt. I don't want to know them anymore; that's it, they're not worth knowing.

The inmates identified two types of people in jail: those continuing to fight the system and those ready to take responsibility for their actions and effect positive change. I asked Michael if he concurs with this.

MICHAEL: I'd say three.

AUTHOR: What's the third?

MICHAEL: They're sort of on the fence, they don't know whether to change or keep going. They want to change but they don't want to look weak to their mates and they don't know how to get over the fence. They're sitting on it and doing certain behaviours that show they want to change, but when they're influenced they'll jump back over this side of the fence, you know what I mean? I was there for a while; I was sitting on that fence for a while.

AUTHOR: What did you see as the push, the final kick?

MICHAEL: For me it was my children, my wife and myself. They wanted me to change a long time before I actually did.
  My daughter will be eleven when I get out ... I was eleven when my father came and picked me up and all I can see is that I've inflicted my whole life on her through my behaviours, my actions. And had I had that time again that would never happen. At the time maybe I didn't know what I should have known and I can't change time. All I can do is make the most of what's left.

Several inmates stated that prison incarceration may have been a blessing in disguise, an opportunity to finally deal with pent-up emotions. Jason discussed his experience, describing how the shock of jail and the length of his sentence provided him with the impetus to re-examine his life. Had he not gone to prison, he believes, he would not be alive today.

JASON: If I hadn't come to jail I would have been dead for sure. At least jail made me wake up and think to myself about what's going on. Before I came in it was party, drugs, on the dole. I didn't care about anyone but myself. Live day by day. I didn't ever think about the future. When I look back, I was heading nowhere, [was] on a merry-go-round going around in circles and never getting anywhere.

That's the beauty of jail: you've got plenty of time to think. Makes you stand back and have a look at who you are and where you're going and where you've been. I don't think jail is the answer but it can be positive to some people.

For Jason, the change in his attitude came midway into his sentence. He began weight training and reading self-development books, then found religion through an outreach Christian program—Kairos Prison Ministry—run in some prisons.

JASON: It took about four years before the real transition happened in my life. I started training with weights; it was the first time that I'd actually got motivated to go and do something to change myself. And through doing the weights my self-esteem started to pick up ... I had very low self-esteem, very low self-worth. I started reading a lot of books on different religions, self-help books [such as] Men are From Mars, Women are From Venus, *books on Buddhism, Hinduism, different spiritualities. And that's pretty much when it all changed and I started thinking about my life, where I was going and where I've been. Before that it was like I was numb, spiritually numb. I had no empathy towards people. It's like I wasn't really there, I had no emotions. I got to the stage when that wasn't the person I wanted to be and I was sick of it. I didn't want to be a bad person anymore. I didn't want to not care anymore and only think about myself.*

Prison is an emotional journey where your head's up in the clouds and the next moment you are so far down you feel really spiritually bankrupt, like nothing seems to go right. And it's like that all the way through—up, down, up, down. Sometimes it's harder than other times. For me I didn't feel that I was measuring up to who I wanted to be and that made me feel depressed, because I had these expectations of myself and I just couldn't live up to them. Which is understandable; to change twenty-five years overnight is a very hard thing to do.

I ended up doing this Christian program called Kairos they've got here; it's a program designed to help people and I thought, 'Oh well, I'll give it a go'. I was a bit hesitant at first because when I walked in there were all these outside people and that was really weird for jail, to see so many civvies come in. Over the next three days what they did is give their testimonials, just talk about their life and how God has affected them. Some of the things they talked about were really amazing. Like, I thought I had problems, and you listen to other people and the positive way they dealt with their problems and how God came into their lives. And I felt something I'd never felt before, which was love—I never had it in my life when I was younger—and I couldn't stop smiling. I smiled for the three days; my jaw was sore. It was unreal.

I found that in the Church there are a lot of good people. The majority of people are good. One of my goals is to create a positive network when I get out. Encouragement: that's the key to success; to have people behind you to give you that push when you need it. As a kid love is what I was missing from my life. My favourite bit of the Bible is the story of Joseph because he was the outcast of the family and he had a lot of things to overcome and he always kept a positive attitude and ended up becoming a leader.

Behind David's poker face and cool exterior lay fear— fear of his own nightmares—which led David to seek change and enrol in the VPP. It was during our last visit that he relayed these thoughts and, although I could not be sure, I felt he was taking a chance and letting his guard down.

DAVID: I came here because I got sick of seeing all the blood, I had enough of it because I had nightmares about it. I can't have my TV off because I'd seen faces and things like that. And I've had people die right in front of me, seen heaps get stabbed, seen heaps get electrocuted. I used to love looking at people's eyes, the way they drop and hit the ground; I used to laugh about it and now it's affecting me. It gets to me a lot.

I think I might be just getting older in me mind, growing out of my teenage ways. That scares me— sometimes I get scared to go to sleep—I've just had enough of seeing the blood and that. It's getting to me; it's really, really getting to me.

I don't let me mates know about that. I tell one of me mates; he's in for murder and I talk to him every day ... We used to, when we were two-out, we used to practise fighting with knives, where to get people—in deadly spots, you know, instant death—and I'll tell him, 'Fuck, I've been having these nightmares', and he goes, 'I am too but I've been having them a lot longer'. It's getting to both of us and we both just got sick of it, so we said,

The Revolving Door

'Let's see if we can do something about it, let's get out of it', then we decided to come here.

This is the first jail where I haven't been walking around with two knives on me; it's the first jail I don't shower with knives. Normally I shower with a knife in me mouth if I'm in Goulburn or Bathurst. I walk around in thongs in this jail; I can't walk around in thongs in other jails. I just said to myself, I've had enough, you know, the killing and stabbing.

AUTHOR: How common was this type of violence?

DAVID: Used to be, like, a stabbing every day, probably a killing every fortnight.

AUTHOR: Have you grown tired of it? Is it enough?

DAVID: It scares you, what you put your body through. Like, when I was a teenager I couldn't ever imagine stabbing a bloke and laughing at him and, when he's hit the ground, looking at his eyes going, 'You all right, mate? You all right? No, you're dying; see you later'. That's jail; its reality.

You can't relax in jail. Me mates—when I was two-out— they will say I sleep with one eye open. As soon as I hear the keys I'm up straightaway, me shoes are on. That's the first thing I get on ... my socks and me shoes. Always have me shoes on when the doors open so I'm on me toes, I can move around a lot better. You've always got to be on your toes, you've always got to expect the worst. Like when you fight: be prepared to fight to the death.

I respect blokes ... who say straightout they can't fight. I'll help them out who says, 'I can't fight but I'll have a *go'. When I see him in trouble I'll help him out. It's funny, I'm starting to get a soft spot for some people.*

Something happened a while ago: a couple of blokes were standing [over] this bloke for $16,000 and they thought he didn't know no-one, and this bloke come up to me and the older fella and told us what was going on. He told us he had to pay it up within two weeks or something would happen to him. We looked at each other and I said, 'Look at him, he's harmless'. I said, 'I'm pretty mad, you know, them trying to stamp him'. I don't like things happening in jail if I don't know about them. We … looked at each other and [said], 'Let's stamp them, see how they like it'. So me and me mate went out in front of them and told them we want their buy-ups tonight—if not, we're going to get you the next day. They're running around trying to get their mates together and no-one wanted nothing to do with it. And we're laughing at 'em and that. So we saw them again at night-time and said, 'Bets are clear then; you don't owe us nothing if he don't owe you nothing', and they just left us. He just made us feel sorry for him. These are the blokes that we used to stand over like three, four years ago and here they are doing it to other people. We can't let that happen. If anyone is going to do it it's going to be us. Me and me mates, we don't like letting nothing slip past us, we want to know everything what's going on and when something slips past and we find out later, we get dirty.

Once inmates are released from prison, their ability to succeed in life on the outside depends on many things; none more so than a support network of friends, family and others to aid the transition. The effects of spending years behind bars and moving between jails in various parts of the state, however, mean that most relationships have faded and need to be re-established, or let go.

> *SHANE: My daughter is now eleven, and she's experienced quite a lot of trouble because of the way she's been raised. She's such a gorgeous little girl and it's been such a shame that her life has been such a shambles at such a young age. Last Christmas was the first time I'd seen her since she was five years old; my father brought her out and we spent all morning together. We stay in contact now but it's very hard for me to tell her what to do in her life because I'm not available. I look at what I'm about to say and I think, 'Well, who are you to say that?'*

Stuart is unsure what will happen to his relationship, which was placed on hold when he began his sentence.

> *AUTHOR: Do you keep in touch with your girlfriend?*

> *STUART: No, I haven't spoken to her for about three months. So I don't know; I mean, she's got a life. I have a son with her but whether she finds somebody else, well and good. But, I mean, if that opportunity arises when I get out, I will still follow it up. But I will be realistic about it. If I believe there's no future in the relationship I'll end it straightaway because I believe it's only hurting myself and hurting her.*

> *MICHAEL: I'm lucky. I don't know about other people, but for me, I've been with my wife since I was seventeen,*

and out of the thirteen years I've been with her I've been in prison for over ten of them and she's been there for me, and we have an understanding and a connection and she knows when I'm doing it hard. I'll ring up and I'll talk to her or I'll write her a letter. It helps me a lot to write it on paper, how I'm doing and that, and I'll deal with it that way. Only in the last four years or so I've learnt to talk to psychs and share my troubles and that, and I didn't understand at the time how it would help me. But I'm pleased to [have] met this psych in '97 over in Twelve Wing and I just felt relaxed with him and I wasn't usually like that.

AUTHOR: Were you suspicious?

MICHAEL: Yeah, and I didn't even know why; it's just the way I was brought up. White people: some can be trusted but a lot of them can't be trusted. Look what they've done to us.

AUTHOR: Do you speak to your mum?

MICHAEL: Yeah, all the time; not all the time, [because] she hasn't got the phone on. She just finished working at the medical centre where she worked for eight years. I could ring her at work but now she doesn't work so I haven't spoken to her for about seven months. I've spoken to her on the phone when she goes to my wife's house, very rarely. But my children—I've got three—my mum sees them every day.

AUTHOR: One of the things I've noticed is that Koori inmates have a deep respect for their mums, for all mums.

MICHAEL: Yeah, it's just a bond. Mum's always there for us. Just that indescribable feeling about being Aboriginal, you know what I mean? It's just the way mums are, it's just respect. It's hard to describe. My mum was a heroin addict from when I was little and she was an alcoholic before that; she didn't even look after me [but] I still love her, like, heaps.

AUTHOR: Do you get on with your dad?

MICHAEL: Yeah, I ring him every week. He lives up the coast and he sends me birthday money and Christmas money. I ring him every week to see how my little sisters are going, how he's going.

AUTHOR: What's the most important relationship in your life at the moment?

MICHAEL: My youngest daughter; she's about ten; she visits me here. I ring her every day. Sometimes I don't speak to her, some days she's at school, some afternoons she'll be out playing, so I'll miss her.

AUTHOR: Are you more connected with her than with your other kids?

MICHAEL: The other kids are with another mother ... so I don't get to speak to them that often. Last time I got to see my eldest daughter was about four months ago; my current wife brought her out here.

AUTHOR: What do you talk to your daughter about?

MICHAEL: How she's going at school, make sure she goes to school, behaves for her mother; what she does after school; who she's playing with; how her cousins are, 'cause she knows all my family and she plays with her cousins; see how they're going, how my wife's going. 'Cause my wife's got two little kids, too, they're [my daughter's] sisters.

AUTHOR: How did you meet your de facto wife?

MICHAEL: I've known her since I was a kid.

AUTHOR: Were you seeing both mothers of your daughters at the same time?

MICHAEL: Yeah. Eleven years ago she was in a relationship with her first children's father, and I was in a relationship. We knew the feelings we had for each other but I did nothing about it. But then the inevitable happened, so they split up and I split up, sort of thing, and we got together ... her youngest [daughter] was only nine months old.

AUTHOR: It sounds like you've changed a lot; how did your partner react to these changes in you?

MICHAEL: It was hard for her at the start; it caused her to act a lot differently 'cause I wasn't the same person, and she was, like, freaking out. I suppose it was hard for her but I just kept persevering through it and trying to support her as best I could. She's slowly coming around and I've seen my behaviour slowly rubbing off onto her. Positive things.

AUTHOR: Did your relationship with your kids change after you came to the VPP?

MICHAEL: Yeah, definitely. My children never used to like coming to visit me in jail. But now I'm able to help them through the duration of the visit, like, keep them occupied and motivated mentally.

I started seeing that my behaviour is making my wife and children victims—making them look at me through glass and they couldn't hold me when they wanted … I just decided I had three years to go and I've got to start now 'cause if I fall somewhere along the way I'll still be in jail and I'll just have to pick myself up and learn from it.

I knew in my head that I had to start with the drugs. I knew that I couldn't think rationally if I was still going to use drugs because they were first and foremost on my mind the whole time instead of what should have been. And so I started with them and from that also a lot of other things, like with this program: it's shown me [how] to look at other things in life and deal with them, just soul-searching my own thoughts and that. And I always wanted to stay out of jail and have known what I have to do to do that but [was] not feeling very confident about it. This place has given me the confidence, plus skills.

My self-esteem is one thing—I know that's the highest it's ever been. I used to have high self-esteem but [also] negative stuff; just for positive stuff it's something that I've never felt before and now I'm feeling it at such a high level.

AUTHOR: What kind of life are you going to have with your kids when you're released?

MICHAEL: *Hopefully a more positive one. I've been doing a lot of group work and it revealed how I picked up a lot of my father and mother's behaviours as a child without even really knowing it. And it's helped me realise that if I'm going to be a negative role model, then [my children are] going to pick that up and pass that on to my grandchildren and their children. Whereas, if I'm a positive role model then, unawares to them, they'll pick up those positive attitudes and behaviours … I'm hoping for a happy time with them. Whatever time I have will be spent with them, making their life happier than the last twelve years.*

AUTHOR: *What do you hope for your kids?*

MICHAEL: *I hope they just get an education first and foremost; that whatever field they choose to go in, whether it be sports, whether it be business, whatever, that I can help them and that they can succeed in that. And just that they're happy, respectful and responsible adults.*

AUTHOR: *Can you express emotions to your kids? Do you tell them you love them?*

MICHAEL: *Yeah, I tell them every day on the phone.*

Gordon married his wife while serving in Lithgow jail and, like Michael, has sustained the relationship.

AUTHOR: *How long have you been married?*

GORDON: *Eight years.*

AUTHOR: How did you get together?

GORDON: When I was out last time, or, when I was on the run last time, that's when we got back together. The feelings were still there, they were still as strong as ever, but I always had that with girlfriends, but she's special, you know, [my] soul mate. You can search a lifetime and never find them and then you can look down the street and there they are.

AUTHOR: How do you sustain a marriage in here?

GORDON: Listen, if you can maintain your relationship through this, then you being out together is nothing.

AUTHOR: How do you deal with the separation?

GORDON: Through much perseverance, mate; like, sometimes I wish no-one was visiting me. I've always been an isolationist, right? I love being by myself.

AUTHOR: Do you have any kids?

GORDON: One kid, we've got one son. He's eighteen.

AUTHOR: What kind of relationship do you have with him?

GORDON: Well, he knows what I've done; you can tell that there is pride there, like, 'Yeah, my dad's a fucking bank robber, yeah', and I've shown him, like, gun safety.

AUTHOR: Are you encouraging him to go into your line of work?

GORDON: No, I'm encouraging him to get jobs. But he's like me at his age, really; could go either way.

AUTHOR: Can you talk to him?

GORDON: Yeah. I tell him I love him every time we finish talking on the phone: 'I love you, mate'; 'Love you, too'.
  I never brutally fucking belted my kids, either. I'd give them a smack on the arse once but that's the extreme punishment, you know, a smack on the arse.
  We've got to be mates, right? That's where the strong relationship comes from. Like, if he thinks of me as Dad then there's that different relationship, you know? He doesn't have to love me; he loves me for who I am, I love him for who he is. He doesn't have to love me because I'm his father.

AUTHOR: It's more of a mateship?

GORDON: Right, that's what it is, that's what it needs to be.

I also asked David about his relationship with his children.

DAVID: My kids? One's sixteen—I had him when I was a teenager—one's eight years old, one's five. They're good kids. I got 'em into sports. When he was about six I made him do karate for a few years, until he was eleven. I made him do boxing; he still does boxing now, he's a tough kid. The eight-year-old is on his blue belt in karate so I want to make sure he gets his black belt. And I'm going to do the same to the youngest. I just want them to know how to look after themselves in fights.

They're strong Catholics. I was a strong Catholic, used to go to church and sing in the choir and all that. Now my kids go to church Monday and Wednesday. I don't let 'em swear, nothing like that. 'God's children', my mum says.

AUTHOR: What kind of contact do you have with them?

DAVID: I ring 'em, like, every second day, see if they're going to school and stuff like that. Since my girl passed away my sister has got custody of them, and they verbal me sister because she's a couple of years younger than me, she's about twenty-six. They're good talkers, mainly the eight-year-old; the five-year-old is like me sister's little boy, calls me sister Mum and that, but the others try to verbal her. That's why I have to ring up every second day and talk on the line, let them know she's the boss and that.

AUTHOR: Do they listen to you?

DAVID: Oh yeah, they're terrified of me. I don't have to tell 'em nothing; it's ... the way when they come out and see me, just the way I look at them. Sometimes when they've been doing wrong I won't talk to them for around twenty minutes, I'll talk to me sister and I'll make them sit down there. Then I'll start talking to him, 'Why are you doing this?'

AUTHOR: Are you scared that your son will end up going to jail?

DAVID: Yes. Then I'll have to come back to jail, to look after him.

In families in which tension has been a norm, some relationships are irreparable. Darren feels there is no room for him in his brother's life.

AUTHOR: What's your relationship with your brother like?

DARREN: We used to argue a lot. I'll always love the bloke. I don't particularly like the bloke, but I have to love him I suppose, he is my blood. Haven't seen him for a hell of a long time. It's very sad.
  He's had two children and I'm basically not allowed to see them because I'm a criminal. And it's hard because I know I've got a niece and a nephew but I can't contact them. [It's] not so much my brother but his missus—she won't let me see them. Mum buys them presents and [my brother's missus] takes it back to the shop and gets the money and stuff like that. It's very spiteful.

AUTHOR: Is your brother in contact with your mum?

DARREN: No. All because of his missus. He'd rather have his woman than Mum, which is fine but if he ever turns up on her doorstep he'd get hurt. That's the way it's got to be, make him realise it's his own goddamn mother. This woman put breath into you, she give you life, for Godsake. He sided with Dad; he's still with Dad. He was with Mum but I think Mum might have talked bad about Dad all the time and that maybe hurt him, and I went the opposite way, I went back with Mum.

Of all the inmates, mild-mannered Jason appeared to have the best prospects for the future. With a healthy and realistic attitude, support from two of his siblings and religious faith offering him communal connections, things looked bright.

JASON: I'm feeling really excited about getting out but, then again, a bit cautious, I suppose, a bit scared. I've been in jail a long time; nine years is a long time and my transition to the outside hasn't been great. I've only had two day-leaves [and] I haven't had a chance to do work release, so I'm sort of just going to be out there all of a sudden. And I don't know where I'm going to fit in. Like, jail is easy; everything is done for you, all your decisions are made for you. And that's going to be hard—start going to do everything for myself. I am lucky, I've got two good sisters out there who are very supportive and ... will help, and I've got some Christian friends that will help as well; that support network is very important. I think the tattoos will give me away, especially being covered in tattoos. Maybe I'll get a bit of discrimination through that.

AUTHOR: When you think of being out, what images come to your mind? Where do you see yourself?

JASON: I think of myself just walking around the streets. Sometimes I'll walk around the yard and I'll think, 'What's the feeling going to be like walking down the street with all the people around?' I'll take one day at a time. I love the bush and nature, so I'll probably go to the Blue Mountains and that, and I'd like to start a business in the future. I'll be moving probably a three-minute walk from the beach; I'll sit on the beach and just play my guitar and watch the waves rolling in. Things like that you miss a lot. It's going to be a lot different than in here.

AUTHOR: What about your family?

JASON: I haven't spoken with my parents for twelve years and I know it's going to be hard confronting them but I want to go and see them, and if they accept me, at least the ball is in their court. I think my mum wants to see me but my father I'm not really sure. I still talk to all my family; my little brother I haven't seen for a while. I've just seen my older sister for the first time in about five years, seen her kids. They came here on Christmas; that was a good present. I've got two sisters who come in all the time—they're my best friends as well; they're pretty special. The other family—cousins and that—I haven't seen for fourteen years. All I hear is on the grapevine. Maybe I'll go see them as well when I get out.

Life is easy in here because all your decisions are made for you, and that's going to be hard to start having to do everything for myself … I … know it's going to be very hard; it's not going to be easy, no way.

Shane's personal journey will also include a search for his birth parents.

SHANE: I still don't know who my biological parents are but I've done quite a bit of inquiring into it; I've got all the paperwork to initiate contact but I don't really want to do it while I'm in prison. Sometimes I think that I should in case something happened and I never got the chance.

Most of the inmates had modest future ambitions. When asked about work, the inmates invariably—like so many Australians—wanted to run their own small business. But it seemed that the inmates had little practical experience to temper their dreams towards more realistic goals.

SHANE: As for my future, at the moment I'm leaving my options open; eventually do a full work release so I can get some financial stability and get back in touch with what's going on out there. Probably long-term goal I'd like to own my own business, whatever it [may] be. And I'd love to move to Western Australia and settle over there.

GORDON: I'm going to start my own business up. Seriously, I was going to do this as a kid; still think it's a good idea. It's landscape gardening but I've got extra ideas … let's just say it's a full home maintenance service. Then I'll have time on my own; I'll have my own bike—there'll be bikes, yeah.

AUTHOR: You're four years from getting out? Does that seem a short time?

GORDON: Yeah. Well, once I hit Windsor that's when it starts going down, because then I'm coming up to day release, weekend release, work release.

David, although hopeful of keeping out of jail once he's released, was realistic about his future prospects. For him, jail had become home and outside life was simply too daunting. He did not expect his current sentence to be his last stint inside.

DAVID: I spent two-and-a-half years in segro. Six months was the longest. You got your segro, then you got your high-security. High-security means first two weeks you got no electricals, and if you've on good behaviour, if you don't swear at officers, you can get one electrical thing, so that's your TV. You got to stay in the high-security unit for three months and then go to segro. You're locked in your cell in segro twenty-four hours sometimes; like, get out an hour every three days. You have your moments in there but that's the time when you've got to think mentally strong, you can't let the system beat you. You talk to yourself a lot; if you've got your TV you watch shows; you get used to it. That's how come the outside scares you a bit— there's too many people out there.

AUTHOR: Do you think you'll come back to jail?

DAVID: Yeah.

AUTHOR: Doesn't it bother you?

DAVID: It bothers me a little bit but I can't change the way I think over so many years.

AUTHOR: What would stop you from coming back to prison?

DAVID: One of me mates was telling me [that] in America they have a lot of juveniles, that when they get charged the parents have got to do the time and that. If that happened I would stop, if my mum and dad had to do the time or something like that. I guarantee, if *they done that here a lot of us would stop. Because that's the only thing we got here: it's our parents and that. That would stop me, definitely.*

AUTHOR: You don't seem to mind prison too much.

DAVID: It's home. The outside scares me. I don't know what I'm going to do. Like, when someone calls me a 'black cunt' on the outside I'll go right off me head. That scares me, it does. I don't want to ... but we got to look at reality.

AUTHOR: You know you'll have to respond?

DAVID: That happens with the police and that; they tell me what I can do and I'll go, 'Right'. All depends on how people treat me. It's all commonsense; if people want to treat you like a dickhead then you treat them like a dickhead— you're forced to. I'll talk to you properly if you talk to me properly but if you raise your voice I'll raise my voice.

I always expect the worst, always do. And that's good; gets you going, keeps you on your toes. I like to be on my toes all the time. It's a hard life out there; no-one respects you out there. I've got respect in jail. Makes you feel good about yourself, it does. It's just a feeling you can't get on the outside. Here it's a home, it's the life, I'm healthy. I do what I want; to an extent I got no worries.

AUTHOR: What do you miss?

DAVID: I miss only little things ... the taste of ham, the taste of chewing gum—I haven't had chewing gum since

'96—just little things. Just watching the water, the birds, sounds of birds; watching kids play around in the park; I miss the little things. Like, to people on the outside it's nothing. I miss—I was saying this to me mate the other day—I miss girls' tongues, the tongue of a girl.

AUTHOR: How long do you have left?

DAVID: Not long; I've been in since '96, so not long at all. I don't know what I'll do yet. I've got three kids; [I'll] try and look after them.

AUTHOR: What's your dream?

DAVID: I want to go up and live in the mountains, like, Byron Bay, and just grow heaps of dope, just kick back. I've got a couple of uncles who own a couple of fishing trawlers up north; might just work with them and then just go back to Byron Bay ... Just be away from everybody because I don't like crowds, never have. Just stay away from people because I like my peace and quiet. I believe in Dreamtime. I don't believe in heaven. I believe we live in hell and the place we go is the Dreamtime, back to our totems.

All of the inmates also spoke of a desire to give back to society, to make amends in some way for their past behaviour, and seemed sincere when expressing this. The most common intention was to help other young people avoid the inmates' mistakes.

GORDON: I'd like to go and lecture at night-time at different places to young people ... I've been put here on this planet for some purpose and I believe this is it. Not to do my time and live my life in jail but to start helping other people stay out of it.

JASON: Something I've been thinking a lot about is how I can give something back to society rather than taking. I'm not sure, but maybe something to do with young people, help them. The best would be to help really young people before they do things. If somebody is starting to go down the path where they are rebelling, I think they'd find it a lot easier to talk to somebody like me because I've been in jail and I've done the things they're starting to do. My life has definitely been a lesson in what not to do. But I really believe I can become a productive part of society.

AUTHOR: Is that why you agreed to speak with me?

JASON: A few people asked me what you're doing here and why I'm talking to you. I tell them this is my chance to share with people what I've gone through and that might help somebody.

Through friends I was introduced to a mother of a former inmate who told me that her son, after serving a five-year sentence, took some time to adjust to a life of freedom. Even walking on carpet needed to be re-learnt after years of treading on linoleum. 'Sometimes I would find him standing at our front door, waiting,' she said, 'waiting for someone to unlock it for him, something he hasn't done for himself for several years'.

Jason seemed most realistic in his assessment of the future.

JASON: I figured, it took me a year to get used to jail so it will take me a year to get used to the outside again, maybe even longer. I've heard [that] the people who find it the easiest in jail are the ones who find it the hardest when they get out, so I hope that's not true. The good thing with jail for me is that it's taught me a lot of skills.

Chapter 7:
Final Thoughts

Over the two and a half years I visited with inmates in Long Bay jail, I was glad to leave prison each and every time. I found that as I walked out of the prison wing and towards the car park my pace would quicken. My time with inmates taught me that the only people who wish to remain in prison are institutionalised inmates who cannot find anything better to do or anywhere else to go.

Interestingly, once I had adjusted somewhat to the constant noise and the blandness of prison architecture, I began to notice how calm everything seemed on the surface. And the more I learnt about the tense undercurrent, the more striking the contrast was. In truth, the prison environment cultivates the worst of human traits.

The inmates I met did not simply wake up one morning with violent and criminal tendencies; theirs was a long apprenticeship, with prison the likely outcome. For some, incarceration was an expectation of their peer group, for others, it was even an ambition.

Violence was behaviour they learnt early in life from their fathers, and which was reinforced throughout their childhoods. It is only in recent years that the pivotal role that fathers play in their sons' development has been spoken of widely; a dysfunctional relationship with their fathers was a common thread in the stories of all the inmates I interviewed for this book.

The inmates' emotional development was stunted from an early age due to their unsettled home environments, and they found solace in alcohol and drugs. With few boundaries, no positive influences and much frustration to vent, they were lured by crime and violence—it is, therefore, not overly surprising that they ended up where they are now.

The crimes the inmates committed over the years were grave and left many victims. However, it is important to understand that when we put criminals in prison, while we may satisfy our punitive urges, the inmates do not learn appropriate emotional responses and behaviour, nor are they equipped for their imminent release into the community. They are housed in a morally bereft society that merely reinforces their violent tendencies; and however angry they are on entering prison, many leave even angrier—and it is society as a whole that bears the brunt.

Only a small number of people are imprisoned for the remainder of their lives, and it can be argued that there is no point in rehabilitating such inmates as it is unlikely they will ever be reintegrated into mainstream society. All other inmates, however, are eventually freed from prison; most having served sentences much shorter than the inmates featured in this book. The type of people they emerge as ultimately depends on whether anything has changed in their mindset and behaviour during their incarceration. It also depends on the place of incarceration, the environment they are placed in and the opportunities it provides to facilitate and encourage change. Even more important, perhaps, is the support structure that awaits them on the outside, dictating whether they build a new lifestyle or continue their old one.

The inmates featured in this book have shown that our prisons are tense and high-pressure environments that lack any sense of safety or security. They are societies in which violence is the norm, where displays of strength are the primary measure of success and where vulnerability and emotional expression are despised and derided. The reality of our prisons is that experienced, stronger and well-connected inmates prosper while weaker and younger inmates are targets for abuse.

Official attitudes to rape and brutality in prison are a cruel joke and somewhat Kafkaesque. The lack of formal complaints by inmates is cited by officials as proof that no problem exists. But inmates are, of course, in no position to make such complaints, as the consequence of implicating a fellow inmate can be fatal. We have also seen that sentencing some inmates, particularly the younger and leaner ones, to maximum-security imprisonment can be utterly destructive and inhumane

The Violence Prevention Program is an island of contrast to the prison norm. Here inmates that are ready to change the destructive course of their lives are encouraged to recognise and confront their violence, its origins, triggers and impact on victims. They can learn to adopt new and more appropriate modes of behaviour in social interactions. They are encouraged to express their emotions and are shown that in doing so they do not diminish their masculinity.

However, the VPP is an exception to the rule, and the program can only cater for a small number of inmates for a limited period of time. Those who graduate are not then placed in a position to practise and hone their newfound skills, but are returned to the general prison population where survival requires them to suppress what they have just learnt.

Programs such as the VPP are staff-intensive and a lot more expensive to run then a mainstream prison environment. But considering their potential to reduce recidivism, the short-term costs could well translate into savings in the longer term.

My interviews with seven prison inmates showed me that society is best served by a system that aims to rehabilitate and accepts that incarceration is punishment in its own right. For prison to serve a rehabilitative role, the public must encourage state governments to spend money on progressive programs and not simply assume or hope that society's problems have been solved by incarcerating the perpetrators of crime.

State governments, for their part, should break the habit of the past decade (during which the prison population increased exponentially), and the course they have set for the next, of building more prisons to house more criminals. Otherwise, we will remain trapped in the revolving door syndrome, and the cycle will continue.

Within the context of our interviews I found the inmates friendly, interesting and generally good company. While I was aware that under different circumstances they may have treated me considerably less amicably, I also learnt that behind their destructive natures were emotionally stunted men living out patterns of behaviour adopted early in their upbringing. With their own readiness, realisation and commitment, the will and resources of the government and its agencies, and most importantly, the community's support, a better outcome for society at large is possible.

Most of the inmates I spoke with are still serving out their sentences, dispersed throughout NSW correctional facilities. Shane is scheduled to return to the VPP, this time as participant rather than chef. Darren was released and was to appear in court in the coming months for breaking his parole conditions. On a brighter note, Jason was released some time ago and is doing well.

Endnotes

Prologue

1. Peter Schneidas, *And Not to Yield*, unpublished memoir.
2. The psychiatrist's report formed part of Schneidas's court submission.
3. Submission to NSW Supreme Court hearing for the redetermination of Schneidas's sentence.
4. Submission to NSW Supreme Court hearing for the redetermination of Schneidas's sentence.
5. Unpublished judgment of Justice Grove in Schneidas's redetermination hearing, NSW Supreme Court, 16 December 1993.
6. Submission to NSW Supreme Court hearing for the redetermination of Schneidas's sentence.

Introduction

7. *Life after Life: Interviews with Twelve Murderers*, Harper Collins, London, 1990; *The Violence of our Lives: Interviews with Life-sentence Prisoners in America*, Henry Holt & Co, New York, 1996; *Criminal Conversations: An Anthology of the Work of Tony Parker*, Keith Soothill (editor), Terence Morris (Introduction), Routledge, London, 1999.
8. New South Wales Department of Corrective Services, 'Summary of Characteristics' *NSW Inmate Census 2001*, Statistical Publication No. 23, Sydney, April 2002.
9. New South Wales Department of Corrective Services, 'Operational Report', *New South Wales Department of Corrective Services Annual Report 2001/02*, Sydney, 2002.
10. US Justice Department, Bureau of Justice Statistics Bulletin, *Prison and Jail Inmates at Midyear 2002*.
11. New South Wales Department of Corrective Services, *NSW Inmate Census 2001*, loc. cit.
12. New South Wales Department of Corrective Services, 'Commissioner's Foreword', *New South Wales*

Department of Corrective Services Annual Report 2001/02, Sydney, 2002.

13. David Indermaur, 'Violent Crime in Australia: Interpreting the Trends', *Australian Institute of Criminology Trends & Issues in Crime and Criminal Justice*, No. 61, Australian Institute of Criminology, Canberra, October 1996.

14. NSW Corrections Health Service, *Corrections Health Service Annual Report 2001-2002*, Sydney, 2002

15. New South Wales Department of Corrective Services, 'Operational Report', *New South Wales Department of Corrective Services Annual Report 2001/02*, loc. cit.

16. Julian Borger, 'Warden Who Witnessed 89 Executions', *The Guardian*, 15 May 2001.

17. Gore–Bush Presidential candidates debate, 17 October 2000, St Louis, USA.

18. Federal Bureau of Investigations Uniform Crime Reports, summarised by the US Department of Justice Bureau of Justice Statistics.

19. Roger Hood, *The Death Penalty—A Worldwide Perspective*, 3rd edition, Oxford University Press, 2002, p. 230.

Chapter 1: Meet the Inmates

20. The case citation details have been omitted to protect the inmate's identity.

Chapter 2: A Bad Start

21. Australian Bureau of Statistics, *Australian Social Trends 2002*, ABS cat. no. 41020.0, ABS, Canberra, 2002.

22. New South Wales Department of Corrective Services, *NSW Inmate Census 2001*, loc. cit.

23. New South Wales Department of Corrective Services, *NSW Inmate Census 1998*.

Chapter 4: Welcome to Prison

24. New South Wales Department of Corrective Services, 'Operational Report', *New South Wales Department of Corrective Services Annual Report 2001/02*, loc. cit.
25. ibid.
26. ibid.

Chapter 5: Living in the Jungle

27. New South Wales Department of Corrective Services, *NSW Inmate Census 2001*, loc. cit.
28. David Heilpern, *Fear or Favour: Sexual Assault of Young Prisoners*, Southern Cross University Press, Lismore, 1998, p. 83.
29. Jacquelyn Hole, 'Jail Rape Inevitable: Yabsley', *Sydney Morning Herald*, 22 February 1991.
30. Bill Birnbauer, 'Jail Rape Stats Offer False Security', *The Age*, 20 July 2001.
31. David Heilpern, op. cit., p. 41.
32. A new fine default scheme was introduced in New South Wales in response to the Partlic case. The scheme initially provided for the issue of community service orders, instead of imprisonment, for failure to pay traffic or parking fines. Amendments to the scheme commenced in 1990 to provide for jail terms where an offender has applied for and received a community service order but failed to comply with its terms.
33. Primo Levi, *The Drowned and the Saved*, Simon & Schuster, New York, 1998, pp. 105–206.

Chapter 6: The Revolving Door

34. New South Wales Department of Corrective Services, *NSW Inmate Census 2001*, op. cit., and *NSW Inmate Census 1999: Summary of Characteristics*, Statistical Publication No. 19, New South Wales Department of Corrective Services, Sydney, 2000.
35. David Heilpern, op. cit., p. 171.

Index